Best W.

Malcolm Leary.

Painted
With Pride

The Forgotten Story of How One Woman Taught
the Broken Men of WWI to Live Again

by

MALCOLM LEARY

Dedication To "Painted Fabrics"

This book is dedicated to the memory of the employees and staff of Painted Fabrics who unknowingly provided me with the privilige and opportunity to tell their moving and inspiring story. I have also had good fortune to tell the story my way; no writer could ask for more.

I sincerely hope I have done them and it justice.

The need for the kind of dedication to the concept and practice of a 'duty of care' to those less fortunate than ourselves, through no fault of their own, exemplified here and described by the Painted Fabrics story, is sadly and to our shame still required today and provided by such organisations as Help for Heroes who will be a recipient of net profits from sales of the Painted Fabrics Centenary Book Project.

The making of the story belongs to those involved with Painted Fabrics. They are the history makers.

Any inadequacies or errors in the telling of the story are my responsibility alone.

Malcolm Leary
Hope Valley
2016

First published in Great Britain in 2016 by:
© Malcolm Leary

Editors: Martin Edwards and Adam Kay
Design: Dan Wray

Images reproduced by kind permission of Sheffield Archives.
Additional images courtesy of Wikimedia Commons
and Willequet Manuel/Shutterstock.

Printed and bound in Great Britain by CPI Colour Ltd.
108-110 Beddington Lane, Croydon, Surrey CR0 4YY
Tel: 020 8688 7500
Email: sales@cpicolour.co.uk

A CIP catalogue record for this book is available from the British Library.

ISBN: 978-1-907998-22-5

Proceeds from the sale of this book will be donated to Help for Heroes.

Contents

Even now, in the 21st century, the legacy of the First World War can be seen right across Continental Europe.

It's hard to travel through northern France or Belgium without seeing the cemeteries that follow the line of the Western Front, their endless rows of white headstones stark against the green fields.

But in the immediate aftermath of the conflict, there was another testimony to the human cost that had been exacted by more than four years of war.

It came in the shape of tens of thousands of men, maimed or disabled to a greater or lesser degree, who would carry a reminder of the war every day for the rest of their lives.

It was they who felt more acutely the betrayal of the promised 'land fit for heroes' they had been led to believe they had won the right to expect. It was those men who found it most difficult of all to find a new purpose in life.

This is the story of how one remarkable woman's inspiration lit the way, helping countless numbers to triumph over despair.

It was to be the most crucial battle of their lives. That they won it was due to an unlikely heroine, a socialite-turned-entrepreneur who put her own indelible stamp on the canvas of history.

1

What Can I Do With These!

Bolton Journal and Guardian, Friday 12th November 1926

Courage and Grit

"It was through a Bolton man crippled in the War that the possibility of finding employment for disabled ex-servicemen in the decoration of fabrics was first revealed. The story is one which has irresistible appeal to all who are stirred by examples of courage and grit. In 1916 Mrs Geoffrey Carter [an artist of repute] formed an Arts and Crafts class for disabled men at the Wharncliffe War Hospital, Sheffield. One day by chance in the grounds of the hospital she met Corpl. William Wallwork of the R.F.A, who before the war had worked in a butcher's shop on Bury Road, Bolton. He had suffered terribly in the war; he had been burned by liquid fire and both hands had been amputated. One arm was off at the elbow, the other arm finished at the wrist. His face was also burned. He was wandering in the grounds of the hospital in a distraught state, very depressed, with his cuffs stuck in the pockets of his greatcoat. When she suggested that he might like to join her art class he scoffed at the idea of drawing without hands. His face had a solemn expression and as he pulled his deformed hands from his pocket, his strong words were:-
"What can I do with these!" he declared, holding up the bandaged stumps.
After a good deal of persuasion, he eventually came to the classes.
Mrs Carter was profoundly touched by this incident and immediately set about devising a plan. She began by tying a brush to the stump of one of his arms, then cutting out stencils. She taught him to paint, first on paper and afterwards on cushion covers through the stencils. She knew little about human anatomy but the specially designed tool at least enabled him to do some of the "work."
"I was in despair," he told a Journal and Guardian representative, "Life did not hold anything worth living for, but this work showed me that there was at least something useful I could do. It gave me hope and courage."

2

Annie Bindon Carter's Painted Fabrics

"Neath cold sand I dreamed of death,
But woke at dawn to see
In glory, the bright, the morning star.
This was not judgement day,
Only morning; morning, excellent and fair."

Emily Dickinson

Roll Call

List of some of the men who have found work at Painted Fabrics

NAME	RANK	REGIMENT	NATURE OF DISABLEMENT
SIMPSON, H,	Lance Corporal,	Coldstream Guards.	Amputation of right arm and half left hand; remainder useless
HARDY, A,	Able Seaman,	Royal Navy.	Amputation right arm and left leg
CROOKES, H,	Rifleman,	Rifle Brigade	Amputation left leg. Gunshot wound, right shoulder, causing stiff right arm.
HIGGINS, T,	Private,	Kings Own Yorkshire Light Infantry	Gunshot wound, left hand. Severe epilepsy, Neurasthenic.
COLE, A.J,	Private,	65th Canadian.	Permanent injury to stomach. Periodical seizures, during which he suffers great agony.
THACKRAY, W,	Private,	York and Lancs.	Gunshot wound right leg and amputation of left arm.
GREGORY, H,	Private,	Middlesex Regiment.	Gunshot wound right arm. Paralysis. Gunshot wound left hand.
WILDGOOSE, A,	Private,	York and Lancs.	Gunshot wound in head, and permanent paralysis left side. Silver – plate over wound in skull.
ROSEWARNE, G,	Private,	York and Lancs.	Amputation right arm, Gunshot wound left arm, side and leg.
WHITHAM, W,	Private,	Kings Own Yorkshire Light Infantry.	Gunshot wound head. Permanent paralysis left side. Fits.

GOODE, G,	Private,	K.O.Y.L.I.	Gunshot wound head. Permanent paralysis left side. Fits.
POULES, F.	Private,	K.O.Y.L.I.,	Amputation left arm. Gunshot wounds both legs and side. 37 wounds.
SHOOTER, S.A.	Private,	York and Lancs.	Amputation left arm and right leg. Gunshot wound left side.
COOKE, S.A.	C.S.M.I.	York and Lancs, Sheffield University Officers Training Corps.	Amputation left arm. Gassed.
WALLWORK, W.	Corporal,	Royal Field Artillery.	Amputation both hands and left forearm. Burnt, liquid fire.
GILLBANK, A.	Private,	York and Lancs.	Amputation left arm.
LANHAM, J.W.	MM.A/Corporal,	Essex Regiment.	Amputation right arm, left hand.
RILEY, H.A.	Private,	1st York and Lancs.	Right arm amputated.
VERNON,	R.H.A/Corporal,	8th Gloucester Regiment.	Gunshot wound, left arm.
LLEWELLYN, T.W.	DCM[2 bars], MM [2 bars], Croix de Guerre, Russian decoration, Sergeant,	Welch Regiment.	Amputation left lower leg, Gunshot wound, thigh.

DYSON, H.	Private,	Queen's West Surrey's.	Amputation right arm.
KNIGHT, W.	Private,	East Kent's.	Amputation both legs.
G, RAMSEY,	Private,	2nd Worcester,	Gunshot wound, spine.
HOLMES, J.	A.B,	Naval Division,	Amputation foot.
BROOKES,	Private,	West Yorkshire,	Gunshot wound shoulder.
WALKER, W.	Private,	West Yorkshire,	Amputation right arm and right leg. Also left arm damaged.
CALLAGHAN, B.	Gunner,	Royal Garrison Artillery.	Amputation, both legs.
JOHNSON, A.	Private,	York and Lancs.	Amputation, both legs.
GRINDEL, R.A.	Sergeant,	Coldstream Guards,	Musculo- spiral paralysis left arm.
SIMPSON, A. E.	Sapper,	Royal Engineers,	Amputation, right leg.
WIGGINS, C. N.	Private,	East Yorks.	Amputation right arm.
ELLIS, B.	Private,	K.O.Y.L.I.	Double amputation, both legs. 15 other gunshot wounds.
HARTLAND, A. G.	Private,	Machine Gun Corps 147050.	Gunshot wounds spine. Paralysis.

TESH, A.	Private,	Northumberland Fusiliers	Amputation, right arm.
BOWNES, H.	A.B.	Royal Naval Division.	Amputation, right arm.
LOXLEY A.	Private,	K.O.Y.L.I.	Amputation, left arm.
BROOKES, W.G.,	Private,	Durham Light Infantry.	Amputation left leg.
MARLOW, C.	Corporal,	First/Fourth Northamptonshire	Amputation left arm.
RHODES, B.	Private,	Sixth Dragoons.	Amputation.
MURRAY, J.	Private,	Northumberland Fusiliers	Amputation right leg and left arm.
HARPER, A.	Rifleman,	34th London Division.	Fractured Spine [has always to be laid flat on his back.]
BRITTAIN, C.		Oxford and Bucks,	Amputation, legs from knees.
HAMMERTON, H.	Private,	7th York and Lancs.	Amputation right leg and neurasthenia.
REES, D.J.	Corporal,	2nd Battalion Welch Regiment.	Gunshot wound left arm and shoulder.
RICHARDS, A.	Private,	Argyll and Sutherland Highlanders	Gunshot wound, right arm.
SUTTON, A.J.	Private,	1st Royal Munster Fusiliers.	Double amputation, both legs.
HEMS, H.	Private,	Yorks and Lancs.	Amputation, right leg.
DONOHOE, F.	Private,	1st/5th Docks Operations, Wells.	Amputation, left thigh.

COOPER, G .A.	Private,	York and Lancs.	Blind, one eye, head wounds and facial disfigurement.
FOX, J.	Lance Corporal,	York and Lancs.	Amputation left leg.
DEAN. F.	Private,	4th Machine Gun Corps.	Amputation left leg.
GRAGON. J .E.	Private,	17th Royal Fusiliers.	Amputation left leg.
HENDERSON, J.	Private,	Northumberland Fusiliers.	Double amputation, legs.
BULL, J,	Private,	Manchester Regiment.	Amputation, left leg.
LAWLESS, J .J,	Private,	West Yorks.	Neurasthenia.
ROE, B.,	Lance Corporal,	5th Notts. and Derby.	Amputation, left thigh.

Annie Clara Bindon Carter, the founder and inspiration behind Painted Fabrics, was born in 1883 in Nottingham. She was educated at the Moravian School in Oakbrook, Derby and from there she obtained a scholarship to the Sheffield School of Art, where she was awarded a prize for her mural decorations and her silver and textile designs (whilst working for several firms in Sheffield and London).

She married Geoffrey Cecil Carter, who was then 26 and owner of a manufacturing chemists (Carter and Sons) in 1909 in Sheffield. Geoffrey Carter (known as 'C.C') was a big man who proudly claimed his weight was 16 stones 7 pounds when he joined the army. Geoffrey Carter served in the war as a private with the Royal Army Service Corps in Mesopotamia. He wrote a detailed account of his experiences entitled 'War in the Land of the Two Rivers'. In his words the war was a story of death and sickness. However he survived and did go on to perform an important supporting role in the development of his wife's lifetime's mission.

As was the convention of the day and according to her position in Painted Fabrics Limited, she was addressed as "Mrs Geoffrey Carter". To her close friend the Countess Fitzwilliam she was "Binnie"; to her fellow students at Art College, "Annie Carter"; and the employees of Painted Fabrics, "the men", she was "Mrs Carter."

They lived first at 9 Silver Birch Avenue, Fulwood, Sheffield, and later moved to 23 Durham Road in Leavygreave.

She served as director of Painted Fabrics from its formation and was awarded an M.B.E in 1926 in recognition of her work for disabled soldiers and sailors.

In 1959 she was also awarded an honorary M.A by the University of Sheffield after she had helped set up a foundation to enable them to purchase a collection of rare books.

"The formation of Private Presses Collection (University of Sheffield Library) was made possible with the financial support of two generous women, Annie Bindon Carter and Dorothy May Goodby [Annie's sister]. It is thanks to them that the University of Sheffield holds some very fine examples from private presses from the late C19th to the early C20th. After a visit to the newly built Main Library she presented a cheque worth 1,000 pounds to the Librarian specifically to purchase "outstanding examples of modern book production by private presses, with a more than academic interest."

"Local artist, entrepreneur and businesswoman Annie Bindon Carter is best remembered as the woman who began one of the most successful textile companies in Sheffield. After WWI many of Sheffield's young soldiers, some severely disabled, returned home without any hope of future employment with a life of despair and destitution in front of them. ABC refused to believe that these young men were fit for nothing, so in 1923 she started a small business called Painted Fabrics Ltd. Between the wars Painted Fabrics was hugely successful." Annie Bindon Carter died in 1968.

WHARNCLIFFE WAR HOSPITAL SHEFFIELD

FURNISS SHEFFIELD

Redemption song

"Painted Fabrics, although this title is now a very familiar one, not only in Sheffield, London, England and many places abroad where exhibitions have been held, I suppose comparatively few people know it from the origins as I do."
So writes Phyllis Lawton, who along with Dorothy Carter, Edith Jagger and a few other friends answered Annie Bindon Carter's call:-
"It was in 1916 that Annie Carter asked me to her home to discuss, along with other School of Art students, the possibility of forming an Art class at Wharncliffe War Hospital. The idea was just as an occupation for the wounded when they were able to move about. We decided to

give it a try. A committee was formed, of which I was one, and we all agreed to take certain materials of our own to start with and took out some of our stencils and cut some simple designs as a start. We were able to go on three afternoons a week from 2pm till 4pm (and it took me an hour each way to travel so I had to leave home before one o'clock returning home sometime after 5pm). It was a great success from the start."

From asylum to war hospital

From the beginning of the First World War virtually nothing was available in terms of accommodation, facilities, equipment and above all ideas on what to do to help the thousands of wounded and disabled soldiers who began to return from the front. A small group of young women, art students from Sheffield Art College on the other side of the city, approached Colonel Vincent, head of Wharncliffe War Hospital, for permission to visit severely maimed soldiers. They believed she could speed their rehabilitation if they gave them an interest to relieve their boredom.

These were the humble beginnings of what was to become an inspiring example of 'man's humanity to man' after the unspeakable horrors and atrocities of the 1914-1918 war.

It became a pressing necessity for many of those deeply affected by the sight of severely wounded soldiers to do something to help in some way.

Comforts for the wounded

Practical solutions had to be found, and a start was made in 1915 with the forming of a Committee to provide help for soldiers who had been wounded on the Western front in Sheffield Hospitals. The minutes of the first "Comforts for the Wounded" scheme for Sheffield Hospitals reported April to September 1915:-

"Beyond the list the Committee has received and distributed large quantities of vegetables of all kinds, fruit for cooking (the result of Harvest Thanksgiving Services throughout the town and neighbourhood), game, smokes, invalid jelly, fish, several joints of meat, etc. Special Christmas

fare asked for turkeys, geese, fruit, dates, figs, boxes of sweets, Christmas puddings and cakes. The normal list of food items includes: Teas, Breakfast, Sausages Pork Pies, Polony, Ham, Brawn, Bacon, Potted Meat, Tinned Fish, Fish Paste, Cake, Eggs, Oranges, Apples and Bananas. Garments from the Clothing Department included suits of clothes, Hospital clothing and requisites."

"New motor van which has been presented to the 'Wounded Soldier's Comforts Department, Sheffield by Mr Drew of Raincliffe, Ecclesfield. Miss Sorby, who is in charge of the depot is seen at the head of the car."

Sheffield Telegraph 1914

But for some like Annie Bindon Carter and her Art College friends, this was not enough. They saw uses for the skills and techniques that they as artists had developed which would involve passing them on to others. At first this seemed impossible.

Severely disabled and blighted soldiers from the First World War had been accepted largely on an ad hoc basis for treatment at institutions in Sheffield from 1916 onwards. Many of them were in a desperate situation, with nowhere to turn and no-one to help. They were battle-weary and severely handicapped, with disabled, damaged bodies and tortured souls.

But as one wounded soldier put it, some of them had the 'good fortune' to meet Mrs Carter and her friends. They would receive some solace by coming into contact with this group of young female art students, led by a quite remarkable young woman.

Innocent victims of a savage, unworthy war, enticed by a false, manipulated sense of 'duty' to King and Country, were redeemed (partially at least) by this ordinary but phenomenal woman, the feisty and determined wife of a local industrialist.

The First World War had left countless thousands of innocent victims desperately in need of help, a situation pleading to be redeemed, not by the victims, but by their rescuers, backed by some of those responsible for starting and carrying on the atrocity, far beyond all reason.

This pressing need for these actions, long overdue in starting after hostilities had finished, was painfully slow to be responded to by institutions formally responsible. They only too often reacted with indifference and inaction. Nevertheless the situation provided ample opportunities for some isolated individuals to take on this obligation. Individuals and small groups who desperately wanted to do something to help, and to act positively on behalf of the broken, abused, and seemingly 'useless'.

Phyllis Lawton explains how the Wharncliffe side hospital group started by running classes:-

"The classes were held in the dining room on long trestle tables and in addition to stencilling (which was my department), they had water colour painting, black and white work, pen painting, basket weaving and bead making (specially-cut strips of brightly coloured paper were rolled on a hat pin and varnished, and when dry they were made up into bead curtains or trimmings for lamp shades, etc).

There was a piano in the dining room – someone always used to come to play and often someone would come to sing. Of course the boys all entered into it all with gusto and soon began to show a certain amount of ability in the work and take pride in doing things neatly. After a time they executed work good enough to be sent up to London for an exhibition of work done by wounded soldiers."

As well as their physical disabilities the men had to struggle with all manner of other problems and concerns.

Working classes in the dining room!

"There were of course all sorts and sizes in our 'class'- one of whose size was so big that I tripped over his legs on the opposite side of the table to the one he was working at. He was a Canadian, 6ft 10½in, and when he was in France they had to dig a special section of the trench a foot deeper so that his head did not show above the parapet.
Another "Tommy" told me excitedly one day that his claim had gone through and he would be going back to the pit instead of the front. He was delighted at the prospect – and it struck me as strange that a man would prefer to work down a pit rather than "out there again". It made me feel that "out there" must be very bad indeed."

The young students were remarkably inventive and ambitious right from the beginning, coming up with ideas and solutions to seemingly insurmountable problems in areas where they had no experience or expertise. Furthermore the intervention of young women of a certain class into such a situation must have been severely frowned upon by their families and friends in many cases. If it did it didn't seem to bother them at all. That there might be possible barriers and obstacles to their passionate desire to help "the men" did not seem to enter their mind and if opposition was shown at all, they were already fully committed to the cause.

A cause and a crusade it was too, and nothing was going to stop them. In fact the direct opposite was the case. They began to quickly recruit as supporters and helpers the very people from whom they might have encountered opposition.

Right from the start just occupying the time of the injured men was not nearly enough – they had to see some end product of their efforts, to produce, to make something tangible and useful, and furthermore could be sold, so that extra funds could be generated to support their efforts.

Sale of work

Phyllis Lawton reports:-
"Well we progressed still further with our classes and held our first sale in the lower Cutler's Hall in Sheffield, which was opened by the Countess Fitzwilliam. The first sale of goods was a great success to everyone's relief."

The fledgling organisation which was later to become Painted Fabrics was on its way.

"It was at this sale that Annie Carter first mentioned the possibility of forming an industry for badly disabled men under the scheme of the 'Lord Roberts Memorial Workshops'. She said that she was willing to dedicate her life to such a project- and how truly she has kept her promise.

She had set her heart on receiving recognition and some financial help. The first grant she got was from the Lord Robert's Fund and when Earl Haig came to Sheffield, she showed him round their first workshop in West Bar. He was so impressed with the work and the need for better accommodation that he gave her a splendid grant from the Earl Haig Fund for the disabled. With that they acquired land to build houses close to some disused wartime hangers, which proved very suitable for workshops.

An attractive block of houses were built in the form of flats so that the men without legs could occupy the ground floor ones and those without hands the upper stories."

All the men being 100% disabled

"This meant that they have lost two limbs and have a full pension, so they didn't have very long hours. They all have gardens to care for, so they all have as pleasant an environment as possible."

That is the story of the growth of a real life industry out of the simple desire to find congenial occupation for men who were recovering from wounds and were not very robust. Annie Carter realised that many would never be robust again and that some light occupations would be all that could ever be expected of them.

"I remember doing a long strip poster lengthways on wallpaper which ran:-

ALL WORK GUARANTEED DONE BY WOUNDED SOLDIERS AT WHARNCLIFFE WAR HOSPITAL

It was to be put across a stall of Sheffield work. Another poster I did was in aid of Miss Corby's Comforts Fund. They made a special appeal one week and had a hand painted poster in every big shop in the city, and when they had finished showing them, they auctioned them off at a charity matinee at the Empire. Curiously Mrs Wilkins, our next door neighbour, bought mine without knowing who it had been done by until she got home and saw my signature.

There was a very fine one done by Charles Sargeant Jagger, the famous sculptor. His sister was one of the helpers and as he was at that time invalided home, she got him to do one as well as herself."

Corpl. William Wallwork

"I now wish to place on record what I am sure must be considered Annie Carter's first and greatest personal triumph, respecting William Wallwork whom I have spoken about earlier, a man whose whole outlook was changed after being brought into contact with her.

Wallwork was so terribly injured that he was not expected to recover. His dugout had been blown up and he was the only survivor. He managed to crawl out terribly injured and burnt, but lost both his hands and his face was disfigured by burns. He had been two months in Wharncliffe Hospital before he was able to go about in a wheelchair. One of the boys brought him into the class after Annie Carter had persuaded him to have a look following their meeting in the grounds of the hospital to see what was going on. He was indeed an object of pity, but we tried not to show it. He must have been wearied of being pitied. He seemed utterly dejected and hopeless, as indeed we knew he must be because he was so helpless, and was unable to do anything for himself. I think it upset us all to see him, as it seemed impossible to do anything for him. But Annie Carter evidently did not believe in the word impossible, and she must have thought hard when he had gone, for when he appeared again, walking this time, I saw her suddenly pick up a light cardboard box and some string. Going over to him she asked in a quite matter-of-fact sort of way if he would take the box to a certain ward, and before he got over his surprise she had tied the box to his arm and took it for granted that he would do her bidding. In a sort of bewilderment, he went. I marvelled at her courage. I don't believe there was anything in that box, she had done it simply to make him feel he could be of use.

The next time he came in to see us, we were working together, probably mixing paint. After looking at him intently she turned to me and said, "Do you think we could tie a stencil brush to his bandaged stump and see if he could do any work?"

Again I was filled with admiration at her determination to try and overcome his great disability.

The suggestion was no sooner made than we set about looking for some string and getting a brush onto his heavily bandaged arm, then she put him in my charge, telling me to get a very simple stencil and see what could be done.

So I got a square of linen crash which the boys used to call an oven cloth, and a small square stencil motif, about four inches. After pinning it firmly down I put beside him a saucer of mauve paint (which happened to be mixed and had a good deal of body colour in it making it less likely to run). Then I guided his arm from the saucer to the material and gently dabbed it over the stencil until completed. When I removed it he was astonished at the result. We did each corner in turn and then one in between, until, by the end of the afternoon we had managed to complete the cushion cover. One glance at his face told us we had done much more than that: we had given him renewed hope in life and confidence in himself as he realised for the first time he could do something for himself."

Never looked back

"He never looked back from that day mentally and only missed the class on one or two occasions when he was not well enough to come. His progress was wonderful. Of course a single brush tied on was not enough and Annie wasted no time in having a special leather strap into which could be screwed three or four brushes so that by twisting his arm around he could use several coloured brushes in turn. He got to be able to do delicate work like scarves, which we used to get orders for and sell amongst our friends, and Annie kept the money to give to him when he left seven months later to go to Roehampton to be fitted with an artificial hand (only the right; the left was to remain a stump). Altogether he was nine months in Wharncliffe with the two months before we knew him. One day the matron came around and after watching him at work, I couldn't help saying as she turned away, "Isn't it wonderful when you recall what he was like when he first came to us?" She nodded and said quietly, "Yes, I remember the day he was brought in — he was one of our very worst cases. In fact there was so little hope that the doctors hesitated to operate and felt they would rather leave him in peace. It seemed cruel to cause him more suffering. Then when he did begin to pull round he didn't want to live and wouldn't see his people, his mother, his sweetheart, because he knew he was disfigured and helpless."

I was very much impressed by what Matron had said, as it confirmed what I had always felt: that until we put him to work he had no desire to live. By the time he left us he had made a nice little sum by the sale of scarves and kept it up after leaving Roehampton by doing them at home. His sweetheart stuck by him all the way through and they were married and she came to Sheffield."

Wounded in the workhouse

Phyllis Lawton also did volunteer work at another hospital in Sheffield; again she describes the place, the work and the men in great detail, some pride and a great deal of affection and admiration.

"The 'E.Cs' or 'Golliwog Ladies', or to give us our full title 'The Ecclesall Comforts and Entertainments Committee', were formed to provide teas and entertainments for the wounded at Ecclesall Hospital (as they preferred to call the Workhouse during the war).

Mrs Sorby had put together a wonderful organisation for providing comforts for the men in the 3rd Northern General Hospital (in peacetime the Teacher's Training College) and its auxiliaries in various council schools.

At one time the efforts of Annie Bindon Carter and her Art Group had contributed to this worthy cause –

The SOLDIERS' PERSONAL COMFORTS DEPOT, Leopold Street, Sheffield, on the 5th of November 1917.

Received from Mrs Carter, the sum of Ten Pounds and Eleven Shillings for Sale of Screen."

Hon. Secretary Edith Sorby

– But the scheme did not include the Ecclesall Hospital and it had come to the notice of one of the most active flag day workers, Mrs Ferne, that the men were rather neglected, so she decided to get together a group of ladies to form a committee. As I happened to know her fairly well, as I had sold flags for her depot, she asked me to go to the original meeting at which the society was founded. I was naturally interested in the scheme, and it was much nearer home than Wharncliffe, yet still I felt I must not forsake them, and it was going to take up the remainder of my time. However I agreed to become a member on condition that I was not expected to go more than twice a week, and I was put on the committee right away.

The first question was how we were to raise funds. Even if we could get permission to hold a flag day, we should have to buy the flags, and they were quite considerable then. Then someone suggested that we should beg bits of wool from all our friends and make little woolly golliwogs, and sell these on our 'Flag' day. The idea was decided upon and each member was responsible for providing 1000 golliwogs by a certain date. We could get any number of people to make them of course, and we also got the men in hospital to make them as well. In addition we had some paper ones printed as well, replicas of the little chaps on Robertson's marmalade. We applied for and got permission to hold a flag day, but it was not to be confined to the West End as there was another being held that day in the city. They did try to get the wounded to collect, which proved very profitable (as everyone would give to a Tommy) until several men were found to have tampered with the tins and it was decided it was rather unfair temptation to men who had little money."

Everything stops for tea

"From then on right to the end of the war we were able to provide extras for the men. Mrs Ferne was like Annie Carter in many respects: when they asked you to do something extra you just couldn't say no. As a depot holder on flag days she was splendid, the way she got all the helpers together to rally round.

Every afternoon some of us would go up early to get their tea ready. We used to get their margarine and bread and use the margarine to mix with something savoury to spread on their bread – salmon always being the favourite. We didn't make sandwiches as they could taste the savoury better when it was spread on a good thick slice of bread. When their urns of tea were brought up we put a tin of Nestle's milk in it. We had been given a small pantry to store our provisions in, and we got the shelves nicely filled with 7lb jars of jam and marmalade, large tins of fruit, salmon, sardines, and so on. And each week we had some Davy's potted meat.

I can tell you they were always pleased to see the 'Golliwog Ladies', as we were always called. Usually after tea some entertainment was provided in one of the wards, a concert or a whist drive. We ladies used to sit on the men's beds which formed the tables, and if it was progressive, the ladies had to do the progressing, except for a few men who were up and about.

They were all wonderfully cheery, as wounded men always seemed to be."

Christmas Day at the workhouse

"At Christmas we had a great time. We all helped to decorate the wards, providing them with a real Christmas dinner – turkey, plum pudding and various etceteras – and gave every man a Sheffield knife as a Christmas present. As one man said to me, "I've often heard of Christmas Day in the Workhouse, but I never thought I would spend one there!" I said, "Neither did I!" Yet except when Billy was over in 1917, it was the only Christmas Day during the war I could call a happy one.

And so the good work went on right up to the end of the war, and even afterwards, as naturally the hospitals didn't close down until many months later.

When at last the men remaining were to be drafted to another hospital so that the Ecclesall Institution could revert back to its peacetime regime, once again we treated the men, before their departure to a visit to the Hippodrome to see some topical show. We spent all our remaining cash on them.

Altogether it was a successful venture."

Welcome to Sheffield

During the First World War many civilian as well as hospital establishments were used as hospitals and convalescent homes for sick and wounded soldiers.

These included privately owned as well as public buildings. In Sheffield the Teachers Training College was taken over by the Territorial Force Medical Services, and became known as the 3rd Northern General Hospital.

Wounded men would arrive at Sheffield railway station, be immediately sent to hospital and moved on to an auxiliary hospital as soon as their health allowed, in order to make room at the base hospital for those in need of greater medical attention.

"Very soon we began to get wounded arriving in the city from the Somme Battle [1915].
The Teachers' Training College was turned into the 3rd Northern General Hospital and staffed by consultants from the other Sheffield City Hospitals.
There were soldiers in some of the other General Hospitals too, of course, but there were far too

many of them coming in to be taken by those alone.
As you can imagine, when the men got to the stage of being able to walk around a little in their hospital blue they were made much of and lack for invitations out for tea.
We were very, very proud of our boys."

Marjorie Llewellyn, schoolgirl in Sheffield from 'Forgotten Voices of the Great War'.

A country seat

If they were very fortunate they might then have been moved to one of the many recovery establishments set up on the moorland outskirts of Sheffield's 'Golden Frame', which surrounded its 'Ugly [Industrial] Picture.'

One such auxiliary hospital establishment was Longshaw Lodge, which was the shooting box of the Duke of Rutland, one of the many private houses used to nurse the sick and wounded of the First World War.

In the words of a reporter from the Sheffield Daily Telegraph, it was:-

"ideally suited for such a home, as not only is it within convenient distance from Sheffield, but it is placed in the midst of the health-giving moors and surrounded by beautiful scenery, which will provide a mental tonic to the soldiers who are sent there to recuperate."

Longshaw Lodge first opened as hospitals in February 1915 and eventually over 60 men were accommodated.

Like Wharncliffe War Hospital soldiers came to Longshaw having fought on both the Western Front and in the Dardanelles campaign.

They came from England, Wales, Scotland, Ireland, Australia, New Zealand, Canada and, from 1918 onwards, the United States of America.

Some of the nurses at Longshaw Lodge had been nurses in peacetime but there were also many volunteers 'doing their bit 'to help the war effort.

There was certainly plenty to keep the soldiers occupied with card games in the smoking room, a gramophone and piano for those with a musical inclination, and the billiard table which had been left for use by the men.

The soldiers could also enjoy plenty of fresh air by walking in the estate, boating on the lake or simply sitting in the garden and enjoying the view.

Country outings

Visitors from the local community used to visit the soldiers, and Longshaw being not far away from the most well-to-do areas, would sometimes take them for trips in their motor cars.

Mrs Alice Clifford (wife of Charles Clifford, whose father was one of the original proprietors of the Sheffield Telegraph) took them back for tea at her home in Whirlow, near Sheffield.

They visited local beauty spots and places of interest including Haddon Hall.

Pte J. C Foster, 1st South Staffordshire Regiment, wounded at Festubert on the 29th May 1915, wrote:

"Many thanks to our sisters for the way in which they have looked after us and many thanks to Mrs Clifford also for taking us on motor rides for our health. When I think that when the ladies are being taken out in the country for moor rides it shows they are all doing their share for the King and Country."

Your True Friend

J.C. Foster

On with the show

The soldiers and staff also enjoyed entertainments given by local performers, as excitedly reported in the Sheffield Telegraph:-

"OPEN AIR CONCERT - The Wounded Soldiers at Longshaw"

"The wounded soldiers at Longshaw Convalescent Hospital were entertained yesterday by a number of artists from the cast of the Sheffield Empire. The event was the first of its kind to be held at Longshaw Lodge.

The entertainment owed its origin to the happy thought of Mrs Clifford of Whirlow, who for some time has taken a deep interest in the hospital.

Mr I Stewart, manager of the Empire, arranged yesterday's admirable concert, which was given in the courtyard of the institution. Mr Stewart had spared no trouble and a fine stage with awning was erected, and every effort made for the comfort of both artists and spectators.

The audience greatly appreciated the diversified programme which was submitted by Mr Neill Kenyon, and included Bruce Green, Athos and Collins, Colts Brothers, the Symphony Girls and the Brothers Vimm. Practically the whole of the Empire Orchestra were present and played the accompaniments for the performers. Mrs Clifford kindly provided tea."

Painted Fabrics forged many close connections with other rescue organisations which formed an important network of support for the plans of Painted Fabrics, including an unlikely one on the South Coast.

Bournemouth Disabled Sailors and Soldiers Workshops

After the end of the war various organisations who had committed themselves to helping ex-servicemen with severe disabilities began to make contact with each other and began to form an informal network based on mutual help and support.

The Disabled Sailors and Soldiers Workshop in Bournemouth run by another formidable young woman known as Miss H A Smith, seemingly another Annie Bindon Carter type of character.

She had started her work for disabled servicemen in 1915 when she began to raise funds from a kiosk on Bournemouth Pier selling woollen garments, soft toys, hand-painted calendars, basketwork and needlework.

Gradually she gathered a small army of helpers, including Major General Sir Harry Brooking, who was to become Chairman of the Charity.

When the Workshop started in 1922 it employed 18 men.

The pay was small and they could not compete with able bodied men. But they retained their pride, self-respect and hope for the future. They produced leatherwork, basketwork and toys.

The Bournemouth Workshops were also associated with the local Toc-H branch, another charity with its origins in the First World War, dedicated initially to giving hope, comfort and respite to men in the trenches, its iconic lamp symbolising a spirit of unselfishness and service to others.

Other organisations Painted Fabrics was connected to included :-

The Disabled Soldiers' and Sailors' Mutual Association,
The National Scheme for Disabled Men,
The Douglas Haigh Memorial Fund and
The British Limbless Ex-Servicemen's Association.

These organisations formed a growing network of hope and practical help in times of great need. Many other establishments were used to help the victims of war, but none quite like Painted Fabrics, certainly in terms of scope and aspiration – and with no-one quite like Annie Bindon Carter in charge!

Whilst most facilities scaled down and eventually closed after the war had ended, Mrs Carter instead moved onto the next phase of her ambitious programme.

Annie Bindon Carter's initiative, which started from humble beginnings in the Wharncliffe War Hospital, later became a well-established business known as Painted Fabrics Limited, its quality products admired internationally and its profile enhanced by support from and association with nobility and royalty. Painted Fabrics was a practical demonstration of progress from the destitution and horrors of the War, created and developed by a woman small in stature but big in heart and her growing band of professional staff and volunteer supporters in an otherwise unremarkable northern industrial town.

This pioneering group immediately confronted head-on the multitude of problems and challenges they faced without a thought for themselves and with a complete and utter dedication to the cause which had somehow presented itself to them. They threw themselves into a complex mix of social, political and personal crises with little or no preparation and not much idea of what they were up against. They soon found out, but proceeded to use this challenge to do inspiring work.

The astounding efforts of Annie Bindon Carter and others went some way to achieving some level of atonement for the actions of others during the war, the individual and collective selfish excesses, indulgences, mistakes and misdemeanours replaced by countless acts of compassion and small deeds of heroic proportions. Crimes against individuals and crimes against humanity associated with The Great War, resulting in agony and despair, to some extent healed by simple acts of kindness, skilled and dedicated help, courageous initiative and personal sacrifice. A small contribution, perhaps, to meet the totality of the needs of the many victims who desperately needed help, but one of enormous significance in the grand order of things. It shows that redemption clearly does not have to come through huge gestures or acts on a grand scale, but in these kind of small, quality contributions as a human reaction to the situation in front of them, actions taken by those who care deeply about what they are doing, take great pride in doing it in the best way possible, and who are directed towards those who are most in need and suffering from life-changing disabilities, as an act of selfless charity, through concrete and specific acts of will. Actions motivated by their own respect for common humanity, particularly towards those who, through no fault of their own, were unable to help themselves, providing countless examples of practical help in terms that the recipients could relate to and understand, find relevant and appreciate and move on using these as a platform for building a different and better life for themselves and their nearest and dearest.

This, then, is the story of Painted Fabrics.

"You may say this is quite impossible"

Annie Bindon Carter once described the tasks performed by the severely disabled servicemen at Painted Fabrics to a Rotary Club audience, as she sought to gain support for her initiative.

"You may say that all this is quite impossible.

I would agree with you … but they can do it.

One man has an artificial left arm and his right hand is artificial. This is covered by a very stiff glove. A hammer can be gripped by his left upper arm and side, and the shaft inserted through the glove into a socket, fixed to his wrist, and with that he can work."

After a pause she added,

"He can also saw".

In the BBC Radio Programme on Painted Fabrics in 2003, Valerie Reid, daughter of one of the co-founders, describes the effects of the treatment methods on one of its early entrants in 1923, Corporal Wallwork,

"He had been blown up and had no hands. He was very depressed and did not want to live. Annie came one day and told my mother to get the simplest stencil she could find.

They tied a brush to his arm and guided it over the stencil. His face lit up and by the time he'd finished he was like a different person."

There is an old saying that all everyone needs in life is something to do, something to look forward to and someone to love.

Painted Fabrics tried to provide these three essentials for a decent living even for those who, when they first joined, felt they had nothing, could do nothing, were wanted by no-one and had no future.

Something to do

The simple but profoundly significant concept that everyone can do something was to become a basic principle of Painted Fabrics work programmes for the men… The men were provided with something meaningful to do, no matter how desperate their condition, by treating them with dignity and the respect they deserved, using amazingly creative new craft and production methods and techniques for them to use, and inviting them to reach out and grasp opportunities created for them and achieve heights that they would not have thought possible, nor would anyone else.

Something to look forward to

And they all had something to look forward to. As Painted Fabrics grew and extended it activities there was always some new sale in which they were often involved, new designs, new product ranges, new ways of working, carefully adapted for their needs, and the odd Royal visit thrown in!

Someone to love?

Some had wives, sweethearts who stuck by them and later children of their own.

And they all loved Mrs Carter!

Something must be done

As part of the rehabilitation programme at Wharncliffe War Hospital, Annie Bindon Carter developed the idea of tying paint brushes to the amputee's stumps. This enabled injured ex-servicemen to stencil fabrics. This was one of the first of ABC's many ingenious ideas for the men to do what seemed at first totally impossible. Annie Bindon Carter is later reported to have said to her audience on one of the periodic visits by local and national dignitaries to the workshops:-

"You will note that a man who has lost both hands cannot feed himself, dress himself or get out of his room, but he can do painted fabrics.

Also in one corner of the workshop sits Mr A. C. Hartland beside a special embroidery machine industriously extending a line newly opened by the company.

Mr Hartland, who served with the Gloucester's and the Machine Gun Corps and was terribly wounded, will tell you frankly what he owes to Painted Fabrics.

Badly shattered with no hope and no prospects, the future seemed black indeed, but his fiancée (now his wife) refused to listen to the gravity of the medical reports. She approached us and arrangements were eventually made for Mr Hartland to go to Coal Aston.

He married and when his wife had acquired surgical knowledge of his case he joined Painted Fabrics. A special machine was constructed to suit his disability and today he is improving in health and doing splendid embroidery work."

After her first efforts were reasonably successful Annie Bindon Carter was set on doing more and she determined to provide more work for badly disabled men under the scheme of 'Lord Roberts Memorial Workshops'. But more opportunities were needed, and she was determined to find a way to provide help.

Premises in West Bar, Sheffield were leased at an annual rent of £100 and a committee was formed. It was agreed that thirteen men would be paid one shilling per hour and work up to 30 hours per week.

A start had been made.

Ladies of leisure

Mrs Carter was described by one of her colleagues as being *"a lady of leisure and reasonably wealthy."*

She was also *"a bit of a go-getter in many ways."*

Phyllis Lawton said unequivocally of Annie Carter, *"I thought she was a great person, as did everyone who came into contact with her."*

Phyllis, who also worked at Ecclesall Hospital, described the two powerful and influential characters she met.

"As I have said before we owed the great success [of Ecclesall] to Mrs Ferne, whose organising

ability I class with that of Annie Carter, two women of vastly different temperament and appearance, one massive, the other frail, but both possessing in a marvellous degree a vitality which they inculcated into all around them."

She also wrote in glowing terms about other staff at Wharncliffe.

"There was another helper at Wharncliffe of whose self-sacrificing work I would like to mention – it filled me with such admiration. Edith Jagger was the girl, and she volunteered to work amongst men subject to fits owing to having head wounds. She had to be locked in the padded room with them and the work they did was practically useless yet she spent time with them simply to take their minds off themselves. She would come up after 4 o'clock and show us some of the stuff they had done and relate her experiences quite unconcerned. It was not at all surprising for a man to have two or three fits in one afternoon. He would be carried off and attended to and presently he would come back and go on with his work as though nothing had happened. You see the reason there were a number of men in Wharncliffe like that was because towards the end of the war the authorities began to specialise to a certain extent and because it had been an asylum and the doctors understood lapses of that kind, they got a number of men with head wounds who required special treatment.

Yes, I think Edith Jagger was a brick, because being an artist herself it must have given her great mental pain to see some of the men's work. Of course that was not the full extent of her work. She did some of the finest designs which were used long after the war among the men of Painted Fabrics and she was on the staff there for a considerable time."

Mrs Edith Jagger was later appointed overseer at £1.50 per hour.

Work not charity

This became the slogan which Mrs Carter began to use to show to people the emphasis on providing real productive and satisfying work for the men, which Painted Fabrics would work towards.

The physical injuries and subsequent disabilities the men suffered were only too easy to see, but difficult to overcome. Once the first hurdles had been jumped, progress in finding some kind of meaningful work situation could be remarkably quick.

Interestingly it was noted that sometimes disabled ex-officers required much more help in finding an appropriate work situation than other ranks.

Mrs Carter observed that:-

"They are, as we have found them generally speaking, unable to do very much normal work in the way of pulling the skips about and so on, and require assistance the whole time. The fit ex-officer as we have come across him is generally speaking a young man who has entered the war straight from Public School, and is entirely unfitted for any commercial work."

The vital first grant she got was from the Lord Roberts Fund. Then when Earl Haig visited Sheffield she showed him round their first workshop at Scargill's Croft in West Bar. He was impressed and recognised the need for accommodation for the men, and in many cases their families. He immediately gave Mrs Carter a grant from the Earl Haig Fund for the Disabled.

The commencement of the enterprise had also been made possible by subscription of a number of local businessmen and later on the United Services Fund had also lent assistance.

All this enabled them to buy land on which to build houses on the old Camp 3 at Coal Aston on the outskirts of Sheffield, close to some disused wartime hangers, which proved very useful for workshops.

More secure workshops with housing nearby was found at Meadowhead and this became Painted Fabrics' long term home. A block of houses was built in the form of flats so that the men without legs could occupy the ground floor and those without arms the upper floor.

From the houses and into the single storey workrooms a network of covered passages were constructed through which men in wheelchairs could reach their benches.

In the workshops they produced dresses, handkerchiefs, headsquares, dressing gowns, house coats and ecclesiastical and domestic wall hangings in patterns and colours "to delight the eye." This became the slogan of the first advertising campaign, and soon word of the venture spread.

Unsolicited testimonials

But to establish the venture on a sound footing was a huge task demanding all the ingenuity and skill they could muster, and all the help and encouragement they could get. They soon got plenty of both.

Letters of support and good wishes were not slow in coming, from a variety of sources, some expected, some rather more surprising.

This must have been a great source of great encouragement to Mrs Carter and all involved in Painted Fabrics.

In 1925 H. Harrington wrote:–

"May I be allowed to send a line to say how much my wife and I enjoyed our visit yesterday to Painted Fabrics. It is difficult for me to express what I really think about it. To think that such work is being carried out by some 40 disabled men in such surroundings with their wives and families beats anything I have ever seen. It was like a tonic to me to see those glorious fellows with their great records in the War doing such splendid work. You could see in their faces how much the men appreciate what they owe you, and no wonder."

In 1935 the General Secretary of the Haig Homes, H.D. Bennett, wrote:–

"Dear Mrs Carter, Thank you very much for your letter and for the really splendid way you have dealt with the case I wrote to you about. I immediately sent a copy of your letter to St James' Palace and they are arranging matters accordingly with Foster and will see that you are informed of the date and time of his arrival in Sheffield. I am arranging for fares etc. and as you seem to have thought of everything, there are no queries from me to discuss with you. I will try very hard to get along to the Imperial Institute before Thursday, however, in the hope of having a little chat with you".

From the United Services Fund (The National Scheme for Disabled Servicemen) on 21st December 1925 a letter came which read:–

"Dear Mrs Carter, It is most kind of you to have thought of sending me a Christmas card and I am really pleased to receive it.

It seems to me though to be quite wrong that you should thank me for anything in connection with Painted Fabrics, as it is more fitting that I should be thanking you for all the magnificent work you have done for so long for the disabled ex-servicemen which I shall never forget".

Fred Terry, the famous English actor and theatrical manager, after his spring tour of 1921 took him to Painted Fabrics, wrote:-

"I only hope that I may be able to put some work in the way of your very admirable firm.

I doubly congratulate you in the fact that your scheme gives employment to those who deserve so well of every Englishman, and this without thought of gift or charity.

Yours is a magnificent institution and I sincerely trust that it will go on growing and gaining in strength. Of course you are exceptionally lucky to have so clever a designer as Mrs Carter, and the gift of her services is invaluable.

"I can only wish her good health to continue the work which does her so much honour and others so much good".

Broken in war, now expert peacetime craftsmen

29th January 1928

Dear Mrs Carter
Enclosed you will find 10 shillings of my debt to you. I am sat here trying to think how I can thank you for all your wonderful kindness. The first of your kindness to me is making it possible for me to have enjoyment for I am a lover of good music and through your kindness I was able to listen to the whole of one of the programmes yesterday. It really is beyond me to express my thanks.
The second of your great kindnesses is your fighting for me, as you know I don't complain but my spirit is getting a little broken now. But when I see we are not altogether forgotten, it puts a little fresh aspect on things. I hope you won't think me impertinent or trying to flatter you but really believe me: we, that is my wife and I, fully realise what you are doing for me.
Believe me I am always your obedient servant.
Taffy Williams, Painted Fabrics

3

Oh! What a Lovely War

-The Citizen Soldier's War

A child of the times

It is inconceivable that the story of Painted Fabrics could be told outside the more general context of the First World War, for it reshaped and changed forever the social as well as political conditions and circumstances within which ordinary people lived their lives.

It altered the way that people of all grades and levels thought about themselves, each other, their community and class as well as other communities, unknown and perhaps even unheard of alongside whom they would live and die.

It changed and transformed everything through the power, passion and impact of WWI experiences, at the front and at home.

Painted Fabrics was a child of these extraordinary times.

When the lamps went out in Europe

The Great Powers of Europe had been engaged in nationalistic tub-thumping and jingoism for years. This, coupled with the utterly stupid alliances and the never-ending agitation of the Kaiser over his lack of colonies ("We want our place in the sun"), meant war was inevitable.

Sir Edward Grey, the British Foreign Secretary realised this, and he commented to a friend, "The lamps are going out all over Europe, and we shall not see them lit again in our lifetime."

World War One, The Great War, was fought over four long years mainly across an insignificantly small area of land in Northern France and Belgium: the farmland, rural landscape and small towns of Flanders, Arras, the Somme and Verdun.

These locations, much like many of the places where the volunteer citizen soldiers and seamen came, from all too quickly were transformed from rural peace and solitude to cauldrons of pain, suffering and futile death. The names of these blighted places evoke the worst of humankind forevermore: Mons, Passchendaele, Arras, Loos and the Somme, Chemin des Dames and Verdun. These unfamiliar, strange, foreign sounding names soon came to be regularly mentioned in despatches and letters home to family and loved ones. The War became deposited on the doorsteps of homes in many a street in the ordinary towns like Sheffield and struck terror into the hearts of communities where the eventual residents of Painted Fabrics would come from. The soil and landscape of their homelands and the bloody battlegrounds of their nemesis formed a painful contrast but also a hideous symmetry.

Battles may have been fought on some 'foreign field', but the 'terroir' of the 'Flanders Fields where poppies grow', must have looked to many new soldiers remarkably like their own home patch. These most humble and ordinary men of the First World War were to experience some of the most gruesome and traumatic events possible for anyone to endure in those few short months and days, and those who did survive had then to pick up the pieces of their shattered lives almost totally unsupported.

As the biggest drama of their lives unfolded they were faced with a succession of new and demanding situations to deal with, all of them completely outside their normal life experience. They were innocents abroad, coming from stable, close-knit family units and communities to be plunged into positions which required new skills and relationships, established and maintained under conditions of extreme danger. Extreme experiences of discomfort and alienation were shared and suffered as repeated massive assaults on their fragile bodies and senses. Little wonder then that many buckled under the pressure, could not cope and even if they could hang on somehow, they might still ended up damaged and helpless shadows of their former selves, in desperate need of help and treatment.

The reality of war

The appalling effects of war were far beyond anyone's expectation or anticipation when hostilities began. In the relatively short period before actual battle was joined they had been engaged in almost frantic preparations with precious little thinking about the likely consequences of pushing the situation over the brink.

The lights may have gone out in Europe as some of the more sensitive and aware politicians had declared, but this was no time for morose reflection or careful consideration; it was a case of let battle commence. After the whistle to start the war had blown everyone was anxious to make up for lost time.

A huge army had to be raised, and quickly. The threat of the dreaded Hun, already demonised in the public eye, marching down our street was upon us and everyone had to join in the fun!

PEAK NEWS 2014

"Recently a local community theatre group put on a play which conditions in WWI were vividly portrayed. It all must have been very daunting. The play began with the euphoria of three young men, representing the seven hundred from the district who had joined up with their mates. They were so elated that they had a big task in front of them: to win the war and soon! Much more exciting than the usual short time working in the mills. The lads were also well pleased as they were getting regular good food, and plenty of it, rather than the scraps they got at home. As a result when they arrived home on leave they always looked bigger and heavier. They were getting seven shillings a week and all found. They were glad to get away from their 'lice and ringworm' existence at home.

But what kind of war was in store for the Pals of Sheffield? In the play the ladies are reading the local paper, which, due to severe official censorship is carrying glowing accounts of Allied gains on the Somme, but slowly and steadily, more reliable sources told the townspeople of the grim reality of the massacre.

The epilogue portrays the ladies laying a wreath of poppies in front of a memorial made up of three soldiers, heads bowed and with reversed rifles. They had eventually and finally come to realise the effects of mechanised warfare on the frail human body."

Brian Woodall

It will all be over by Christmas

Recruitment for volunteers to join the small professional army and navy began in earnest. Exhortations and pleas were made to the nation's youth, calls to duty, patriotism, loyalty, community spirit, protection of loved ones and family – even the need to be just like your pals. All kinds of pressures were used and the pleas and exhortations were impossible for most to resist.

These patriotic pressures had been building up for some time. These were still the days of Empire and jingoism, exemplified by the spectacle of 10,000 children in an Empire Day pageant at Bramall Lane in 1906.

Banging the drum for Britain

Here they come with a tap of drum; Sheffield Lads, Sheffield Lads;-
Every boy his mother's joy; Sheffield lads, Sheffield lads;-
One his 'sis would love to kiss; Sheffield lads, Sheffield lads;
And how proud they make their dads; Bless the lads.
Stepping out with limbs so stout; Sheffield lads, Sheffield lads;
Rank on rank of faces frank; Sheffield lads;
Learning arms for war's alarms; Sheffield lads, Sheffield lads;
Up they come to help their dads; Sheffield lads.
Now they pass, a swinging mass; Sheffield lads, Sheffield lads,-
As they go their bugles blow; Sheffield lads;
Rings the street with tramp of feet; Sheffield lads, Sheffield lads;
And who wouldn't, with their dads; Bless the lads

A Street March of the Sheffield Boy's Brigade
Ebenezer Downing 1906

In his comments, the compiler of 'Sheffield in Verse', Peter Machon, notes:

"What a chilling poem this is, not just because of its militaristic tone, but because considering its date, Downing must have been watching many boys who were later to be recruited into the Sheffield City Battalion of the Yorkshire and Lancashire Regiment which was mown down on the morning of July 1st 1916 in the battle of the Somme at Serre. Downing, known as 'T' Stooaker' could never have known what foreboding was hinted at in his prophetic line, 'Learning arms for war's alarms.'"

Volunteer recruitment had created a new generation and breed of citizen soldier, very different from the professional armies of before, recruited from anywhere and everywhere forming groups of young men with close ties to each other, their families and communities.

Citizens of Hope and Glory

Following on from the Sheffield Boys Brigade came the first moves to create a new structured and disciplined volunteer citizen soldiers army to fight the war.

For most of these naive, unsuspecting young men, joining the new citizen army began with a feeling of elation and relief that they had been able to join up with the others, their 'Pals'.

The collective thrill of these lads, dressed up in uniform, taking part in parades through familiar streets in their home towns, watched by proud families, friends and sweethearts, gladly accepting the nation's gratitude and adulation, is palpably etched on their faces.

Joining up was followed quickly by the novelty and sheer physical exhilaration of training and physical exercise, often out in the open air rather than in cobbled streets under the shadow of Blake's dark satanic mills.

The truth will out

They would be stretched to the limit during the process becoming a serving soldier but it was hardly the same as being down the pit or working in a steelworks melting shop. The new recruits soon became proudly fit, skilled and ready for action.

"Anyone working in the steelworks was in a 'protected' job and industry and didn't have to join the army anyway, they weren't allowed. But I think they all saw the Kitchener posters – "Your Country needs you!" – and off they went to join up in droves."

And didn't they look the part in their new uniforms.

Then, for many, came the added thrill and excitement of being sent together to foreign lands, living in close proximity and relying on each other for almost everything – a great adventure for lads who had hitherto never been further than their own community.

But finally, and inexorably, totally unprepared for the grim reality of what they were about to face, they would arrive at the front to become bogged down in the bloody trenches of Flanders, an awful truth which would threaten every aspect of their relationship with themselves and others.

Raw recruits

For all new recruits a rapid fire succession of strange and puzzling, disturbing but exciting, different yet challenging circumstances came suddenly surging towards the naive and unprepared young men who had had their heads filled with notions of duty and patriotism, comradeship and duty, honour and glory.

Field Marshal Lord Kitchener's posters pointed at the potential recruits:-

The war set to music

'Your King and Country Want You' was a popular sentimental song by Paul Rubens sung at the start of the war. It was written as a 'women's recruiting song' to be sung with the intention of persuading men to volunteer to fight in the war. The song was performed by many famous artists including Vesta Tilley.

"We've watched you playing cricket and every kind of game
At football, golf and polo, you men have made your name,
But now your country calls you to play your part in war,
And no matter what befalls you, we shall love you all the more,
So come and join the forces, as your fathers did before.
We want you from all quarters, so help us South and North
We want you in your thousands, From Falmouth to the Forth,
You'll never find us fail you When you are in distress. So answer when we hail you,
and let your word be "Yes!"
And so your name, in years to come each mother's son will bless.
It's easy for us women [people] To stay at home and shout,
But remember there's a duty to the men who first went out.
The odds against that handful were nearly four to one,
And we cannot rest until it's man to man, and gun for gun!
And every woman's [body's] duty is to see that duty done.
With the rousing chorus of:-
Oh! We don't want to lose you but we think you ought to go
For your King and Country, both need you so;
We shall want you and miss you but with all our might and main
We shall cheer you, thank you, kiss/bless you,
When you come back again."

The war to end all wars

In a further exhortation to become a volunteer and join in the war, recruits were assured that the war would probably not even start, but in any case it would likely not last long and it would be the last.

During August 1914, immediately after the outbreak of the war, British author and social commentator H.G. Wells published a number of articles in the London newspapers that subsequently appeared as a book, The War That Will End War.

Wells blamed the Central Powers for the coming of the war, and argued that only the defeat of German militarism could bring about an end to it.

A version of the original, 'The War to End War,' became one of the most common catchphrases of the time.

The phrase was echoed by no less a person than U.S President Woodrow Wilson, who declared the need to "make the world safe for democracy."

Even the Prime Minister, David Lloyd George, is reputed to have expressed similar sentiments when he claimed "This war, like the next war, is a war to end war."

Willing for a shilling

Young men, especially those who were unemployed, jumped at the chance to volunteer. They did so for a guaranteed pay of one shilling per day. They were thus said to be 'Willing for a Shilling". Sometimes they received it, often they didn't.

There were many recorded instances of under age and over age men being accepted as volunteers. As many as 250,000 under 18s are estimated to have served in the British Army during the First World War, as one in ten volunteers lied about their age.

It was not necessary to produce evidence of age or name in order to enlist, so desperate were the authorities to recruit.

Recruits of all ages and backgrounds were assembled for basic training and off they would go, often with great fanfare and pomp in the presence of their nearest and dearest.

The Send Off

"Down the close darkening lanes they sang their way,
To the siding shed, and lined the train with faces grimly gay.
Their breasts were stuck all white with wreath and spray, as men's are dead.
Dull porters watched them, and a casual tramp, stood staring hard
Sorry to miss them from the upland camp
Then moved a signal nodded, and a lamp, Winked to the guard.
So secretly, like wrongs hushed up, they went
They were not ours,
We never heard to which front they were sent.
Nor if they yet mock what women meant,
Who gave them flowers.
Shall they return to beatings of great bells?
In wild train loads?
A few, too few for drums and yells,
May creep back, silent to still village wells
Up half-known roads."

Wilfred Owen

Joining the Colours

There they go, marching in step so gay!
Smooth cheeked and golden, food for shells and guns
Blithely they go as to a wedding day, The Mothers' sons.
The drab street stares to see them row on row
On the high train tops singing like a lark
Too careless gay for courage, singing they go. Into the dark
With tin whistles, mouth organs, any noise
They pipe their way to glory, and to grave
Foolish and young I am, the gay and golden boys.
Singing, always singing

Katharine Tynan

The war comes to Attercliffe in the heart of Sheffield's industrial East End

Cyril Dexter, 47 Ripon Street, Attercliffe, educated at Woodbourn and Hammerton Street Schools, worked in the Smith's department at Vickers Ltd. Volunteer (one of Kitchener's Army), enlisted 2nd September 1914, aged 21. Stationed originally at Pontefract, with 500 other recruits (most of who were of the King's Own Yorkshire Light Infantry). Went into training at Watmer camp Dover and in a month was on the active service list. Crossed to Dunkirk on the 4th October 1914 and then by armoured train to the outskirts of Antwerp.

"Very soon the men were in the trenches in front of the main ring of forts around Antwerp where they were engaged in fighting from Thursday to the following Saturday morning."

VOLUNTEERS WOUNDED OR KILLED IN ACTION

Private E. Brown, 1st. Battalion, Kings Own Yorkshire Light Infantry, 8th May 1915, killed at The Battle of Ypres.

H. Almon Private, Kings Own Yorkshire Light Infantry 10th June 1915. Fought at Hill 60, now missing.

James Askham Private, KOYLI, missing 31st October 1914 of Latimer Street, Attercliffe.

A. Ashton Private, KOYLI, killed in action 2nd July 1915 of 26 Radford Street, Attercliffe.

B. Beasley Private, KOYLI, died of wounds, 6th July 1915.

L. A. Beedon Private, 6th KOYLI, killed in action 14th June 1915.

Sam Blackwell Private, KOYLI, killed in action, of Carlisle Street East, 5th June 1915.

J. Bollington Private, KOYLI, wounded in action in Belgium of Duncombe Street, 29th April 1915.

Edgar Brown Private, KOYLI wounded at Ypres, of Upwell Hill, 5th June 1915.

Wilfred Buffer Private, 2nd KOYLI. Reported missing since fighting at Hill 60, of Attercliffe, 15th June 1915

E. Burridge Private, KOYLI, wounded three times, returned to action, 25th August 1915.

Private Henry Bolland, East Yorkshire Regiment, of Birch Road, Attercliffe, Sheffield, was reported missing, killed on the 20th September 1914. His death is commemorated on the La Fetre-sous-Jonarre Memorial.

Private H. BOLLAND,
East Yorkshire Regiment.
Reported missing 20th September, 1914.

Some of the citizen soldiers of Painted Fabrics

Arthur Fisher was born 22nd June 1884 at 17 Court, Scotland Street, Sheffield. His father was William Henry Fisher and his mother Ellen (née Duke). Henry was a table blade grinder. Arthur Fisher worked for Robert Slack who owned a confectionary works in Scotland Street. At the beginning of the war he was transferred from Slacks to munitions work at Hadfields Ltd where he stayed until he enlisted on the 10th of December 1915 and joined the Royal Garrison Artillery He enlisted as a private but he was soon promoted to a Gunner. When he enlisted he gave his mother as next of kin and his address as 1/7 Albert Terrace Road.

Arthur was 5ft 8in tall and was trained at South Camp, Ripon in Yorkshire. He fought first in Belgium at the Battle of Ypres and was later moved to Bethune in France. Gunner Arthur Fisher, No 143035 of the 254 Siege Battery received a gunshot wound to both legs and was transferred to 54 General Hospital, Aubengne on the 26th April 1918. Both his legs had been blown off by a shell. His life had been saved by a transfusion of three pints of blood freely given by an unknown Scottish soldier who was wounded at the same time.

From the 15th Casualty Clearing Station, B.C.F, France on the 23rd of April 1918 he wrote to his mother:

My Dear Mother,
This is to let you know I am in hospital wounded. I was wounded on April 21st and have had to have both legs amputated below the knee.
You must not worry as I am going along alright now and shall go from here to base hospital and from there to dear old Blighty.
I shall have artificial limbs fitted as soon as the legs are ready.
Dear Mother do not worry about me, as I shall be soon in Blighty.
Love to all. Your loving son.
Arthur

When he first got the news that his legs had to be amputated his nurse reported that his first reaction was to say "How can I tell my Mother?"

Arthur wrote to his sweetheart Annie at the same time:

"Well dear I am so sorry to tell you I got wounded on Sunday, I have got both my legs off up to my knees but thank God that I'm alive. I still have my life and that's more than a good many I can say."

She immediately replied,

"Well I can tell you it was a terrible blow when I got the news of you but do not worry in any way love as I am bucking up now dear as the future is not as bad as it seemed at first and pray to God to give you strength to get over it and get well again. Well dear you must not think that I will turn against you in any way through it — no dear I shall only love you and honour you all the more from it, and I am going to marry you dear as soon as ever it is possible and if it is your wish love I will marry you by your bedside so cheer up dear and when you are well enough to think about this let me know your wishes. As you say you are better off than many of your poor chums."
Annie

The local newspaper later announced:

LOST BOTH LEGS IN THE WAR

"A wedding of more than ordinary interest took place at Walkley Parish Church, the bridegroom being Gunner A. Fisher of the R.G.A and the bride Miss A. Bell of Walkley. Gunner Fisher was horribly wounded in the "Great Push" on April 21st last year, when both legs were blown off by a shell. On May 1st Gunner Fisher was brought to Lincoln Hospital and during 10 months in that institution underwent six operations.
G. Fisher, who is a Sheffielder, was employed at Hadfields, Newall Road, when he joined up. By a collection amongst the workpeople at the works a good sum of money has been raised for this sorely afflicted hero. It is highly gratifying to learn that Messrs. Hadfields have offered G.F a post for life, which will thus remove any haunting fears there might have been as to the future."

Much later when the Fishers had settled in at Painted Fabrics, Mrs Fisher was moved to offer the following advice to someone else who had faced the same challenges as

Arthur and herself through the correspondence columns of a national newspaper. A legless young man in Bristol had written of his despair after a serious war injury and the impossibility of contemplating now marrying his childhood sweetheart. Mrs Fisher wrote:

"I had to face the same problem 23 years ago," writes "Happy" of Sheffield, "My husband and I were engaged during the last war, He was severely wounded in France in 1918 and had to have both legs amputated. We were married when he came out of hospital in 1919 and as that was before he got his artificial limbs he had to be carried in and out of the church and had to sit by my side during the service.

You see I loved him so dearly to forsake him when he needed me most was impossible. He had lost his limbs fighting for me as well as his King and Country. We have a fine healthy girl of 18. We have had our share of trouble, but we have faced it steadfastly together."

John Edward Gragon was born in Batley, West Yorkshire in 1896, the son of John Gragon and Clara Jane. He had an older brother Percy and a younger brother Richard. John Gragon was a wholesale fruit and vegetable merchant and the family lived at 29, Argyle Road, Meersbrook after they moved to Sheffield. John Jnr. was an apprentice turner/machinist with a Sheffield tool manufacturer when he joined the 17TH Royal Fusiliers.

Lance Corporal L.H. Grindel, Coldstream Guards

Archibald Robert Grindel was a regular army soldier when the war started in 1914. He was a boy soldier who joined the Coldstream Guards at 16. His father Joseph was a drill instructor at nearby Charterhouse School so a military life was part of the family tradition. Joseph originated from Rochester in Kent and Robert's mother Sarah, ten years younger than Joseph, from Chatham, also in Kent. Robert, as he was known later at Painted Fabrics, was born in Godalming, Surrey and had two older sisters, Beatrice and Florence, and a big brother Joseph Jr. They lived at 178, Peterhouse Road, Godalming, Surrey.

I have to go!

Some volunteer recruits went to extraordinary lengths to join in the action for King and Country.

Private F.B. Vaughan, 12th Battalion, Yorks. and Lancs. Regiment, tells his story:-

"I said to the boss, 'I want to join the Army, I want to be released from my job'.

So he said to me, 'Here in the steelworks you are doing just as much for your country just as much for the nation, as though you were in the Army'.

'Well I couldn't see myself catching the 8.40 to Brightside every morning and leaving for home in the afternoon, doing little jobs, and all the time my pals were suffering – probably dying somewhere, serving their country! I couldn't see myself carrying on in that particular way, so I said, very sorry but I've made my mind up. I have to go'.

And he saw that I was determined and he said, 'Well then go to the wages office and they will pay you whatever is due to you. But we will not save your job for when you come back and we will not pay your wages whilst you are away'.

I said, 'All right, I accept those conditions'. My mind was made up, and when I finally joined the Sheffield Battalion, Yorks. and Lancs. as Private F.B. Vaughan – all at a bob a day – you know, I was a very happy man.

It was not just a sudden decision to join the Army. My pals were going, the lads I had kicked around with in the street, kicking tin cans or a football, and chaps I knew very well in the city.

And then if you looked at the newspapers we saw that Canadians were coming, Australians, South Africans – they were catching the first available boat to England to get there before the war was over.

Then when you went to the pictures you'd be shown crowds of young men drilling in Hyde Park or crowding round a recruiting office; or it might a band playing 'Tipperary'. The whole thing was exciting and even in the pulpits they eventually decided to come down on the side of the angels and bless our little mission.

I don't know whether patriotism entered into it or not. We were stirred by the atrocities the Germans were inflicting on the Belgians and French.

Then there were the womenfolk, who seemed very keen on the war.

Before long they were wearing regimental badges, little favours in their coats or hats, and they were offering to do what the men had done in civvy life, so that men could be released.

Some of them would stop in the street and say, 'Well, why aren't you in Khaki?'"

White Feathers

For some other pressures were applied:

Rifleman Norman Demuth – London Rifle Brigade

"I was given a white feather when I was sixteen, just after I had left school. I was looking in a shop window and suddenly felt someone press something into my hand. I found it was a woman giving me a white feather. I had been trying to persuade the doctors and recruiting officers that I was nineteen!'

"As well as being given white feathers there was another method of approach. You would see a girl coming towards you with a delightful smile all over her face and you would think to yourself - my word, this is somebody who knows me. When she got about five or six paces from you she would suddenly freeze up and walk past you with a look of utter contempt and scorn."

But the popular song of the day reminded them:-

And the country found them ready
At the stirring call for men
Let no tears add to their hardships
As the soldiers pass along,
And though your heart is breaking,
Make it sing this cheery song:
Keep the home fires burning
While your hearts are yearning
Though your lads are far away
They dream of home
There's a silver lining

Through the dark clouds shining
Turn the dark clouds inside out
Till the boys come home.
Overseas their came a pleading,
Help a nation in distress.
And we gave our glorious ladies
Honour bade us do no less,
For no gallant son of Freedom,
To a tyrant's yoke should bend,
And a noble heart must answer.
To the sacred call of "Friend".

Up to the front

The Sheffield Pals from 'A Long, Long Trail' by Sgt. Arthur Wilson [No 39114]

"The green, green fields of France made an instant appeal for them by then as they were heartily sick of the burning sand and the blazing sun of Egypt. True they were unfortunate in their introduction to this new land, for, as they went through the streets of Marseilles, sleet was falling fast. The mud soon soaked through their boots, rotten as they were from the sun and salt water of the Suez Canal.

The journey from Marseilles was the most uncomfortable yet experienced. The men were packed eight to each compartment in a corridor train. It was impossible to stack all the packs on the racks so most of them had to go on the floor, with rifles under the seats. The journey occupied 52 hours, and as there was no way that anyone could take a full stretch, nerves got very jagged and limbs very stiff. Despite these discomforts, men found real interest in watching the changing panorama of the French countryside and in airing their French on the porters and passengers at the frequent stops.

At one station rum and coffee were provided by the French authorities, but generally the men poured out of the train and persuaded nearby engine drivers to let off steam into their billy cans, so mashing their tea. Washing was confined to swilling under station taps, in tanks or in any other available manner.

Occasionally a loaf of French bread would be bought from the station buffet or a few biscuits or cakes, but the money difficulty arose and change was not too generous when French money was being offered.

At last the journey came to an end and drew up one noon at a junction, apparently far away from any habitation. The 'fall in' was quickly sounded, packs were shouldered and one of the most gruelling marches began."

Then later, but only a few days, totally unexpectedly, the Sheffield Pals Regiment, one day in Egypt looking after the Suez Canal for the Empire, next after disembarking at Marseilles and after a long train journey through France, at 7 o'clock on a bright summer's morning, came the futile storming of German machine-guns below a tiny village at Serre on the Somme, after a night of artillery bombardment which it was promised would eliminate all German opposition. They were massacred without sense or pity.

On the first day of the battle, they had cruelly lost most of their officers and men. Of the 700 who started, only 132 were alive of those who joined the ranks of the Sheffield 'Pals'.

After the enthusiasm of the send-off this came as a shock to the men's families and communities. For the people of Sheffield, and all the other 60-odd towns and cities in the North of England, the reality of the War was brutally and shockingly revealed. They were left bereft and bewildered as they started to come to terms with their fate.

All quiet on the western front

Arriving at the front a new set of experiences awaited the callow, naive, expectant youth who came face to face with the grim, appalling reality of all-out war – a war between two sets of deadly enemies, who were, in fact almost exactly the same in terms of hopes and fears, compassion, comradeship and common humanity.

Victimhood

In reality all parties are, in fact, victims of the machinations and mechanisms of the conflict.

Individual victims coagulate into a collective mass and victim behaviour becomes addictive.

The conflict escalates, driven on by its own mechanisms and creating its own patterns of behaviour, rules and regulations, every one open to constant dispute, further escalation following.

After the Christmas truce of 1914 and the games of football on Christmas Day, commanding officers soon took over and re-established their authority, of course, and made sure there would be no re-occurrence of the truce nonsense by the enactment of a new regulation which made insubordination such as fraternising with the enemy an act of desertion, punishable by being shot at dawn by one's peers and comrades in arms. But for a short time, at the appropriately poignant Christian Festival where the poorest and lowliest, the peasants and the proletariat become the focal point and purpose of the story, the ordinary citizen soldiers take over and become centre stage, if only for a day and never again.

The damage done

First called 'Shell-shock' at the front and later Neurasthenia in official reports, many suffered from a war illness characterised by fits and hysteria. Serious illness for some from no more than the mere experience of continuous exposure to battle, or the threat and possibility of the battle to come.

The mental damage afflicted more and more combatants as the conduct of the war deteriorated. Psychological distortions of combat soldier's personality went unrecognised, unattended to, and untreated away from the anchors and support of family, friends and community. Repeated nightmarish experiences were constantly relived, undigested and unredeemed.

Battlefield spirit of 'all Pals together' with public school-instilled officer loyalty and mess camaraderie quickly degenerated amid private distress and anguish in a climate of unsympathetic comment, ridicule and sarcasm, rumour.

Layer upon layer of tortured thoughts, terrifying experiences, built up through long nights and interminable days with little or no sleep, foul weather, cold and damp, muck and mud took over the personality and distorted the psyche. Day upon day, month on month, season after season, with no respite, no change or resolution or release, the parties and individuals on both sides of the conflict locked together in a hideous dance of death, with partners who were sworn enemies, but in reality were an almost a mirror image of themselves: naive, gullible, trusting and full of hopes and fears, with no escape, little or no respite, no support and a deaf ear and for some perhaps even worse.

Although escaping or avoiding many of the closest encounters of battle and hand-to-hand fighting, senior officers in the war would also have to endure the pressures of decision, action, reaction and further decision-making about issues of death, destruction, advance or retreat all with lose/lose consequences, punishment and loss. Worse, writing letters home to loved ones about the fallen.

Picking up the pieces

The polluted atmosphere of WWI, charged with thoughts and issues of grievous loss, narrow escape, luck and loss, guilt, anger, retribution, revenge, damage and destruction, meaning and confusion, feelings and emotions so passionately and forcefully by those WWI poets who were directly involved in the conflict itself and in many cases were themselves severely damaged by it. The soul of nations as well as individuals were damaged and distorted. They say the French as a nation never recovered from the horrors of Verdun and Chemin des Dames, and when the Second World War came along only too soon afterwards, when choices had to be made. Collectively the French people seemed to assert that when they said 'never again' they meant it. Better abject capitulation when faced with invading German forces once again than face that again.

The (justifiable) desire for punitive retribution and revenge after WWI led to the onerous and counterproductive terms imposed on Germany by the Treaty of Versailles, leading almost inevitably to the events in a punished Germany which in turn led us to WWII.

The war in figures

The theatre production of the musical play "Oh! What a Lovely War" used the theatrical device (for the first time on the stage with dramatic results) of a back screen projection of the raw data of the war whilst the cast performed the songs and ditties at the front of the stage.

Figures and statistics can illuminate and they can hide. In WWI they were largely hidden at the time but caused shock and consternation and revulsion when revealed later.

The most important statistic for a community such as Attercliffe must have been notification of the first casualty.

An Officer and a Gentleman

The war was not just for 'the men' – officers and NCOs could join in…

One school magazine recorded the award of 19 DCOs to old boys of the school and 36 MCs. There was no room in the magazine for anything but the names of the dead – a total of 457 were killed in the war. Teachers of the school's sixth form were finding it difficult to keep their nerve when the names of boys they had so carefully nurtured towards manhood and university appeared a few weeks later in the dead and missing columns of 'The Times'.

The French displayed their Gallic charm, and acerbic wit to show their true feelings about what was going on. Soldiers from different cultures and armies used their wit through song verse and humour to circumvent a rigid and vicious official military and civil system of censorship and iron discipline with cruel punishment against all who showed any sign of indiscipline, any vestige of insubordination or any hint of 'Cowardice in the face of the enemy.'

"La Chanson de Craonne" was a soldier's song, used to insult the stay-at-home gentry. The French authorities tried to ban the song but by that time it had become so well-known that to do so would have made the authorities look ridiculous.

"On the Grand Boulevards [of Paris] it's hard to look at all the rich and powerful
whooping it up.
For them life is good. But for us it's not the same.
Instead of hiding these shirkers would do better to go up to the trenches.
To defend what they have, because we have nothing.
All us poor wretches.
All of our comrades are being buried there.
To defend the wealth of these gentlemen here.
Those who have the dough, they'll be coming, 'cause it's for them we're dying.
But it's all over now, 'cause the grunts are going to go on strike.
It'll be your turn, you rich and powerful gentlemen
To go up onto the plateau, and if you want to make war,
Then pay for it with your own skins!"

Back to dear old Blighty

From an article by Waldemar Januszczak, The Times
"Returning home after a posting at the front was, in theory, a much-needed opportunity for rest
and recuperation and the re-establishment of close relationships with community, family, friends
and loved ones. Only too often it did not turn out like that. Problems could be encountered
associated with returning home during the war, either on leave or through being hospitalised."

For some the return home meant institutionalisation, for treatment and rehabilitation. Imagine an individual soldier, one who might well have ended up at Painted Fabrics, carrying in addition to their grotesque physical injuries the added burden of mental damage, caused by living through an extended period of conflict such as WWI. On the front line day after day, waiting nervously, anxiously, panic-stricken, for the next onslaught. Already tortured by previous experiences and memories of battle itself and those equally damaging interminable periods of inactivity and waiting, even rest and recuperation, even home leave itself ruined by a desperate inability to leave experiences of conflict behind, but mixing again with friends, family, former colleagues, who had no idea.

Private Edmund Blunden, 11th Battalion, Royal Sussex Regiment

"I became increasingly uncertain of returning to England for periods of leave. Of course being welcomed back and sitting down with one's own, and going for a little trot and seeing a few people left that you knew, that was great. Yet not being able to discuss the things which were at the forefront of your feelings, that was difficult, and perhaps we had, over on the Western Front, placed too much emphasis on certain things. I became a bit disconsolate after seeing everything where it should be in its usual corner. And then I didn't like being treated as a man of means just because I had a uniform on.

"But it was chiefly being treated as if I hadn't been there, in all that muck, for all the notice that was paid to me. Such was the attitude in England, but I ought to have known. It was everybody for themselves, in a way.

"And I suppose there was any reason why any one of us millions — because there were 4 million in Flanders and France in the end — should have been favoured with a nod and a bow and a 'Thank you very much', just for having got a bit muddier and more out of touch with good manners than we had been."

Lieutenant E.W Stoneham, Royal Artillery

"My family didn't understand what was happening out there, and I didn't really want them to know about it. So when I was talking to my parents, or my sisters, I had to pretend that it was all very nice out there and I had to describe a world that wasn't real at all. The real world was the one I had to get back to, and I felt no compunction about getting away when the leave was over."

Private Norman Demuth 1/5th. Battalion, London Regiment

"One thing that I found when I eventually got home was that my father and my mother didn't seem in the least interested in what had happened. They hadn't any conception of what it was like, and on occasions, when I did talk about it, my father would argue points of fact he couldn't possibly have known about because he wasn't there. I think this was probably the approach of the public at large. They didn't know how could they? They knew that people came home on leave covered with mud and lice, but they had no idea of what kind of danger we were in. I think they thought the war was sort of one continual cavalry charge; that we spent all day and all night chasing Germans, or them chasing us. Had they realised the strain of sitting in a trench and waiting for something to drop on your head, I don't think they would have considered it was just play. And of course the general idea was that England couldn't possibly lose."

Captain Charles Carrington 1/5th Battalion Warwickshire Regiment

"The trenches were a man's world and when we were on leave, we were in a woman's world. We found that however pleased we were to see our girlfriends, we couldn't quite get through, however nice they were. If the girl didn't say exactly the right thing we got curiously upset. You got annoyed by the attempts of well-meaning people to sympathise, which only reflected the fact that they didn't understand at all."

As Painted Fabrics' Phyllis Lawton reports, when soldiers returned home from the front, especially if they were suffering from wounds, disturbing nightmares and upsetting memories recalling incidents from the immediate past, their otherwise high spirits at being home and in a safe environment were muted.

"They were always wonderfully cheery, as wounded men always seemed to be. There was only one period when they seemed utterly depressed and too exhausted to enter into anything and that was after Passchendaele in October 1917. They were all badly gassed as well as wounded, many of them being totally blind for a time, and they were so dejected that I found my own spirits drooping."

A war of words

After the war was over many commentators from very different backgrounds could scarcely hold back from expressing their opinions about the war, no longer being constrained by the etiquette of silence about war conditions, the true nature of hostilities and their political and social background.

The Pity Of It

At root and bottom of this, who flung this flame?
Between kinfolk, kin tongued even as are we,
Sinister, ugly, lurid, be their flame,
May their familiars' grow to shun their name?
And their brood perish everlastingly.

Thomas Hardy

Smile, Smile, Smile

Head to limp head, the sunk eyed wounded scanned.
Yesterday's Mail, the casualties, [typed small]
And [large] vast booty from our latest vast haul,
Also they read of cheap homes, not yet planned.
For, said the Paper, 'when this war is done the men's first instinct will be making homes.
If we got nothing lasting in their stead.
We rulers sitting in this ancient spot.
Would wrong our very sleeves if we forgot
The half limbed readers did not chafe.
But smiled at one another curiously
Like secret men who knew their secret safe.
Pictures of these broad smiles appear each week.
And people in whose voice real feeling rings
Say, how they smile!
They're happy now, poor things.

Wilfred Owen

It was as if there was a quiet and unannounced preparation for the flood of men who were to return home as a new breed and generation of victim: the survivors of war.

Poetry of the Great War

No group of artists have managed to express the range and depth of experiences, the overwhelming feelings and raw emotions and the traumas of all people and groups involved in The Great War than a relatively small group of combatant poets, especially Wilfred Owen, Siegfried Sassoon, Ivor Gurney and others. As serving soldiers themselves, it was they especially who were able to represent the ordinary soldier. For some reason poetry has become the artistic medium most closely associated with World War One, even at a localised level, as illustrated by the many poems and rhymes based in Sheffield which are included here, describing particularly graphically the lead-up to the war in social and community terms.

The poetry of WWI describes the thoughts, feelings, emotions and experiences, which the men of Painted Fabrics could recognise.

Some poets focussed on a particular aspect of the war (sometimes changing focus as the war altered direction and emphasis), other times examining a specific issue or cause.

Amid the 'foul-smelling mud, the perpetual noise and the ever-present fear of dying' there was another tragedy which affected many soldiers in the First World War: the wanton devastation of the natural landscape around them. Ivor Gurney, a soldier with the 2/5th Gloucester Regiment, wrote from near St Quentin on the Somme to his friend Marion Scott on March 10th 1917:-

"You cannot think how ghastly the battlefields look under a grey sky. Torn trees are the most ghastly thing I have ever seen. Absolute blight and curse is on the face of everything."

Gurney was a young musician making his way as a composer at the Royal College of Music in London when the war broke out.

He was appalled at the devastation of the land caused by the war in France and 12 days later he wrote a poem entitled 'Trees'. In it he explained the difficulty of remembering the Cotswold beech woods when confronted with the nightmare landscape of the Somme battlefields:

"The dead land oppressed me; I turned my thoughts away, And went where hill and meadow Are shadowless and gay.......Let my thoughts slide unwitting To other dreadful trees...."

He later wrote one of the most poignant pieces of poetry to emerge from the Great War, in which he dreams about and yearns for his home surroundings, its places, aspects and atmosphere. The result is a poem about his home, "Gloster", which could be readily ascribed to every other combat citizen soldier who had a different one, even dear old Sheffield.

The poem was later set to music by Underwood, and sung in Gloucester Cathedral by Bolsterstone Male Voice Choir in front of Joanna Trollope, Laurie Lee and the Ivor Gurney Society as part of the Meningitis Trust's fundraising campaign.

The Fire Kindled

God, that I might see
Framilode, once again.
Redmarley all renewed
Clear shining after rain.

And Cranham, Cranham trees,
And autumn hues
Portway, under the moon
Silent, with freezing dews.
The star of afterglow,
Venus, on western hills
Dymock in Spring,
O Spring of Home

Mayhill, that Gloster dwellers
'Gainst every sunset see
And the wide Severn river
Homing again, to the sea.

Here we go sore of shoulder,
Sore of foot by quiet streams,
But these are not my rivers
And these are useless dreams

Ivor Gurney

Gurney's homecoming was not an easy one. Like many returning soldiers he failed to find work or housing in the chaos of post-war Britain, the lasting trauma of War and the injuries suffered affected his ability to settle back into civilian life, and in Gurney's case this was compounded by the return of the mental illness which had plagued him before the war.

Ivor Gurney died in 1937 in Dartford Mental Asylum. His war poems are specific to the moment, recording the everyday experiences of war for the average soldier. But they also include a deeper message about the human capacity for destruction of the natural environment, and about the wounding emotional and psychological effects this has on those involved.

World War One poets as a group have been criticised for being too sentimental and naive about the war in their work – after all it was a war so what did they expect? But they were there – and earned the right to express their thoughts and emotions their way.

The art of war

The chaos which characterised the war was reflected in the minds of those who were caught up in its savage complexities. Chaos was the First World War's defining condition and this was the characteristic which artists of the time captured, concentrating in many cases on the situation pervading on the frontline involving men in the trenches more than any other.

The ghastly field hospital in Dunkirk, nicknamed "The Shambles", painted by C.R.W Nevinson, an orderly with the Red Cross who shipped out to France in 1914, tells us all we need to know about conditions endured by injured troops.

There were artists amongst the troops in the trenches and they couldn't help but try to capture what they saw and experienced. And it is the eyewitness element of their paintings which makes all the difference. For the first time people were viewing evidence from the front line, and it was profoundly shocking in its bleakness and sensuality.

Nevinson reported that the Dunkirk Hospital smelt of 'gangrene, urine and French cigarettes'. What he saw at the front burnt itself on his memory and jolted all his certainties. What must it have done to the troops? When his health failed he was sent back home, where he set about producing some of the most vivid, searing and profoundly disturbing art ever made, such as 'Bursting Shell', produced in 1915, with its pulsing, driving jet of jagged lines and vivid colours; the physical sensation of explosion experienced over and over again by the troops in the trenches during a bombardment, driving them to certain madness. Like many of the First World War poets, painters were also frontline troops, which gave their work total authenticity. Paul Nash also found himself at the front in 1917, a second Lieutenant in the Hampshire Regiment. His views of the barren and devastated fields and broken trees rising out of a desolate landscape accurately reflect the grim reality of Ivor Gurney's words.

 Killing people is one thing; killing the landscape is another. The spectacularly desolate primeval landscape, entitled sardonically, 'We Are Making a New World', shows us what happens to justice, hope and patriotism once chaos, absurdity and tragedy take over. He wrote to his wife in November 1917:

"I feel I am a messenger who will bring back word from the men who are fighting, to those who want the war to go on forever. Feeble, inarticulate will be my message, but it will have a bitter truth, and may it burn their lousy souls."

Nash's brother John served in the Artist's Rifles. In his painting, Oppy Wood, he depicts two soldiers in the trenches gazing out at what is left of nature once war has trampled across it. In 1917 Nevinson painted one of the most controversial works of the war, a gruesome view of two dead soldiers lying face down in the mud, which he sarcastically entitled Paths of Glory. The official censors refused to let him exhibit it on the grounds that it would 'hinder the war effort.' The picture was bought later and put into storage before anyone could see it. Perhaps his most poignant painting in the context of Painted Fabrics was the one entitled 'La Patrie', a study of wounded soldiers and their conditions.

Nevison also courted controversy when he painted a clumsy, lumpen group of soldiers, from 1917. The squaddies in trench coats were seen by the artist as 'British working man in khaki.'

These portraits were seen as highlighting British degeneration and therefore not worthy of showing. These critical views prompted a riposte from a serving soldier, who wrote:

"Show it to any fellow who has inhabited a dugout ..... You will hear 'Good Heavens! He has got home there right enough'."

Percy Wyndham Lewis's painting of a British gun battery being shelled by the Germans could have been called 'shellshock'. Lewis had witnessed a mechanised death raining down on a degraded humanity; the sudden lethal explosions, the soldiers scurrying panic-stricken underground.

Trench art

Some artists of the war were ordinary serving soldiers who overcame their lack of formal art training, producing drawings, pictures and artefacts of art from artefacts of war. They transformed base materials such as empty shells, chiselled and carved with the most primitive of basic tools into detailed, graphic and exquisite items which are with us today as so called 'Trench Art'.

Decorative items were made by serving soldiers, prisoners of war and those injured or disabled and their art was directly linked to the circumstances, conditions and consequences of armed conflict. Common materials and articles which were used were wood, bone and shell and bullet casings.

Trench Art was a product of the trenches and its beauty is a testament to the indomitable spirit and resourcefulness of the kind of men who ended up at Painted Fabrics to help turn designs seemingly created by folk from a very different background and artistic tradition into products of value and artistic worth.

In 'With machine gun to Cambrai', George Coppard talks about pressing his regimental buttons into the clay on the floor of the trench, then pouring molten lead from shrapnel balls into this impression to make replicas of the crest. This was trench art personified.

Chalk carvings were also popular with contemporary postcards showing carvings into the rocky outcrops around dug-outs etc., which again confirm the existence of trench art in the battle zone. Alongside items that by their nature had to be made in situ, there were also many smaller items such as rings, paper knives, carvings and memento of all shapes and sizes, made by soldiers either in the front line or in support trenches, especially in quieter parts of the line or rest areas behind the lines.

In a foretaste of what was to come in Painted Fabrics, wounded soldiers would be encouraged to do certain craftwork as part of their recovery and recuperation process, with embroidery and simple forms of woodwork being common.

Coppard recalls that, whilst he was recuperating from wounds at a private house in Birkenhead, "one kind old lady brought a supply of coloured silks and canvas and instructed us in the art of embroidery. A sampler which was produced under her guidance so pleased her that she had it framed for me".

Oh! What A Lovely War on stage

It began as a war of words and slogans, but the Great War was also played out as on the stage of the musical theatre. In a blaze of publicity and a flurry of artistic activity, the words and accompaniment of the coming war were recited, sung and shouted from the rooftops.

Subsequent phases of the war, which dragged on after the initial 'It'll be over by Christmas' feeling, were conducted to the accompaniment of more muted and sombre tones.

This contrast between theatrical playfulness and grim reality was later to be played out on stage and in film in the musical play "Oh! What a Lovely War". The popular songs of the day were performed in front of a huge back screen which showed the statistics and figures associated with death and destruction, the amount of ground gained, positions altered and advances repulsed, to create a dramatic music hall atmosphere.

'Oh! What a Lovely War' originated as a radio play by Charles Chilton in 1961, and was based on Alan Clark's book, 'The Donkeys.'

1963 a Stage Musical version was produced at the Stratford Theatre in the East End of London by Joan Littlewood and in 1969 a film version was made by Richard Attenborough. In both the company sang with great gusto:-

"Up to your waist in water, Up to your eyes in slush.
Using the kind of language that makes the sergeant blush.
Who wouldn't join the Army? That's what we all enquire.
Don't we pity the poor civilians, sitting by the fire?
Oh! Oh! Oh! It's a lovely war
Who wouldn't be a soldier eh! Oh! It's a shame to take the pay
As soon as reveille is gone. We feel just as heavy as lead,
But we never get up in the morning till the sergeant brings our breakfast in bed
Oh! Oh! Oh! It's a lovely war!
What do we want with eggs and ham?
When we've got plum and apple jam?
Form fours. Right turn!
How shall we spend the money we make."

4

The Men Who Had Seen Too Much

- Survivor's song

Andy Bell of the Daily Telegraph tells the story of his grandfather, Edwin Vaughan:

"In one of the photographs dated 1916 he stands with his back ramrod straight.
He stares at the camera with the self-confidence of a man who has not yet fired a shot in anger.
In another, taken in 1918 he appears somehow distracted, a man who has seen far too much."

The forgotten army

Survivors from the citizen soldier's army did not want to talk much about their experiences when they returned home. It was left to others to remember, and for them to try to forget.

'Lest we forget' was the all too familiar mantra and slogan of the living for the dead. In practical terms it became only too easy for non-combatants to forget because everyone else seemed anxious to do so.

There are good practical reasons for this. There are few remaining sources of concrete, accurate information. During the London Blitz of the Second World War, official papers and works of Art were quickly secreted to deepest rural hideaways well outside the capital. But they did not escape Hitler's bombers. Thousands of records of common soldiers of WWI were left in a warehouse in Southwark, only to be incinerated into unknowable history.

As a result countless family members and loved ones are left with unanswerable questions. What did my granddad do during the war? Where did he go? Who did he meet? What did he see? What did he experience? And how has it left him? Why was he like he was when he came back?

Albert Edward Leary of Birch Road, Attercliffe, and Sheffield volunteered to join the King's Own Yorkshire Light Infantry at the beginning of the war. We don't know why. He didn't talk about it to his family and they didn't ask.

No records exist to show what he did for the rest of the war, where and when.

As he was 36 when war broke out we can assume he was used on non-combatant duties and his service medal, awarded in 1921, has him working with the Labour Corps.

Besides these official records, sparse as they are, there are a few anecdotal scraps of information to build up a more complete picture of his war experiences.

His daughters – he had four in all – remember him coming home on leave in puttees, talking of a pal called Mick and a place called Arras. He must have been around at home sometime in 1916 for his daughter Irene was born an appropriate time later. His sons never spoke of such things, and never asked questions.

There is a surviving small memento in the shape of a mounted scimitar sword, inscribed with the place name Rouen, which would tie up with the work assigned to the Labour Corps at the main port supply route to the Western Front. As for the rest, nothing.

No mention in despatches, regimental records or official documentation to tell the tale. If any had existed it was burned in the fire at Southwark. So much for "Lest we forget" in Albert's case.

Albert Edward survived the War, somehow, still a Private. He returned to his family in Sheffield and died in 1934.

The dead, the living and the living dead

By 1932 the sufferings of the war seemed to fade in the collective memory, something best forgotten and certainly not discussed – after all, a new one was on the way.

Painted Fabrics' own London-based magazine 'The Sasmatian', was not noted for anything but positive sales-generating news about Painted Fabrics and the war-damaged employees who worked there felt it had to make a comment in its editorial: *"The war and all that it left behind in human suffering is almost forgotten and one only observes occasional references in the newspapers to the disabled. This would appear to indicate that 14 years after the war, disabled men who were national heroes in 1918 are no longer interesting news to the British public."*

Lest we forget.

For some survivors of the war, peace offered no redemption, no respite, no home fit for heroes, no promised land, but instead a life racked with doubt, guilt, tortured by demons who would not be dispelled and carrying the burden of crippling injuries and loss of limbs. They had to somehow find the will to survive and carry on.

Slowly the traumas, injuries and disabilities wartime conditions had caused began to be better understood, by some individuals and agencies at least.

Men who had seen and experienced too much began to be the subject of serious attention and considered research.

Reports on Mental Health and WWI

"Broken men – Shell shock, treatment and recovery in Britain 1914-1930"
by Fiona Reid
"The language of mental health in WWI."

Mental health problems as a result of war experiences were initially described collectively as shell shock, a condition resulting from events such as those described graphically by Siegfried Sassoon:-

"Since 6.30 there has been hell let loose. The air vibrates with the incessant din – the whole earth shakes and rocks and throbs. It is one continuous roar; machine guns tap and rattle, bullets whistling over our heads."

The men who were categorised as suffering shellshock often had symptoms of hysteria, disorientation, delusions, and were subject to bouts of limb paralysis and mental exhaustion. 'Soldier's Heart' was a disparaging term alluding to a lack of effort, or perhaps what we would call chronic fatigue syndrome today – used by Freud to describe a fundamental disorder in mental functioning. This condition was also more sensitively labelled as 'severe fatigue'.

Author Philip Hoare's report on the chequered history of the Royal Victoria Hospital in Netley, Hampshire – the largest military hospital ever built – involved sifting through the archives of a hospital that once housed Wilfred Owen. Hoare delved into the primitive and sometimes brutal world of medicine during the First World War. The most unnerving findings were the reminders of the callous treatment of shell-shocked prisoners.

Officers on the other hand tended to be described as having 'neurasthenia'. When this condition became common amongst the well-educated and officer class it was given a more euphemistic title: 'environmental', caused by 'bad experiences'.

In 1917 the term 'shellshock' was no longer allowed. Men were classified N.Y.D.N or Not Yet Diagnosed Nervous. The men called it Not Yet Dead Nearly. The intention behind the innocuous-sounding acronym was clear: keep this man in the line, he's not dead yet.

Terms used for mental illness on the 1911 Census form include imbecile, idiot or lunatics, the places they were incarcerated madhouses and asylums.

Shellshock and neurasthenia were terms the military found it difficult to deal with.

Shellshock was often felt by many to be another term for cowardice in the face of the enemy.

Officers were afforded more enlightened treatment in small, specialised clinics, such as Craiglockhart in Scotland, as described by Pat Barker in her Regeneration novel series. Men too traumatised to re-join society were taken into hospitals run by the Lunacy Board of Control to be 'snapped out of it'. Or they were left to wander around the grounds of hospitals such as the Wharncliffe War Hospital, Sheffield where they might have the good fortune to be discovered by Annie Bindon Carter.

Mrs Scott-Hartley, Voluntary Aid Detachment from 'Forgotten Voices of the Great War;'

"I was working as a V.A.D in a hospital in 1917 in Bulstrode Street in West London. It was a big house taken over by the authorities, and all the cases were shellshocked, which meant that they couldn't keep their hands or heads still. I had to hold them gently behind their heads and feed them."

War combatants who returned, having somehow survived, were almost immediately identifiable by the horrendous visible injuries they were struggling with.

On the other hand many war survivors suffered very different treatment.

Masculinity, shell shock and emotional survival in WWI

With the urgent needs of the military taking precedence, there was little scope for restorative treatment in many cases.

It would be a battle the men would have to fight even after hostilities ended. The experience of traumatised soldiers meant they were in a constant struggle to restore themselves in work and family life.

After the war was over, things would be different, said the optimists. Indeed they were. As the focus shifts to the post-war period, the predicament of the 'hysterical' ex-soldier becomes more and more apparent as we find evidence of their struggle to gain respect and assert authority over their diagnosis and their memory of the war – as well as, in many cases, their severe physical difficulties.

When studying the soldier in the post-war world we find the men themselves have a very different set of goals. Complex realities were faced by actual men who were desperate to salvage their sense of masculinity and restore their sense of honour as legitimate war victims in a seemingly disinterested world.

Many responsible institutions and individual made worthy efforts to first of all help the men themselves recover their self-respect and sense of independence.

Wilfred Owen writes about men "Whose minds the dead have ravaged." As a consequence nightmares, tremors and other disturbing symptoms followed.

In the higher echelons of military and civilian circles the perception was that all this was a distasteful subject best forgotten.

From below, for the shattered men, living symbols of a futile, disgusting war, and the broken communities they came from, the traumatic memories were impossible to forget or run away from. There was some anger when it was found that some men had become economically destitute or trapped in insane asylums. But most authorities remained frustratingly insensitive to the victim's complex problems.

They were called 'war neurotics' in Germany, and in France, the 'walking dead.'

A question of guilt

THE GUILT OF THE VICTIM
Although guilt has been described as the 'unnameable' feeling and emotion of the First World War, there are many references to its existence and influence. Guilt had a place in the damaged psyche of the First World War.

THE GUILT OF THE RESCUER
In Ford Madox Ford's 'Parade's End', Major Tutijens guilt at the death of one of his men in front of him is palpable and haunts him. He wished he could have done more.

THE GUILT OF THE PERSECUTOR
The guilt of T.E. Lawrence, 'Lawrence of Arabia', in David Lean's film is palpable after the unprovoked attack of a Turkish column retreating from Baghdad has him joining in the massacre with the chilling order to take 'no prisoners'. Lawrence's cruelty towards the Turks is thought to be based on the desire to be revenge for his abuse at the hands of a Turkish Officer after his capture. Was this cruelty followed by

guilty feelings? Remorse? The need for redemption? Perhaps there was rarely time for such luxuries under the conditions of World War 1.

Pat Barker's 'Eye in the door' considers the prison (mis)treatment of a female conscientious objector who protects and shelters others.

Did conscientious objectors feel guilt at not having played the same part in the war as the rest of their families, friends and neighbours, perhaps even their 'Pals'?

The Survivor Comes Home

Once in a blasted wood, a shrieking fevered waste,
We jeered at death, where he stood
I jeered, I too had a taste O' death in the wood.
Am I alive and the rest Dead, all dead? Sweet friends.
With the sun they have journeyed West;
For me now night never ends. A night without rest.
Death, your revenge is ripe, Spare me! But can death spare
Must I leap, howl to your pipe Because I denied you there?
Your vengeance is ripe.

Robert Graves

Back

They ask me where I've been,
And what I've done and seen.
But what can I reply,
Who know it wasn't.
But someone just like me
Who went across the sea.
And with my head and hands,
Killed men in foreign lands.
Though I must bear the blame,
Because he bore my name.

Wilfred Gibson

The Survivor's Guilt

"I should have gone back."
"Why did I leave him?"
"It should have been me!"

The 'guilty' may feel remorse, and need to obtain forgiveness, sensing the need for some kind of restitution.

Serving soldiers often reported that so-called 'Battle Nightmares' included feelings of guilt.

The term 'guilt' has clearest indications of one of the emotions and feelings often felt by survivors, but visible evidence of its manifestation is questionable. Guilt works away in the deepest and unreachable recesses of the psyche, eating away insidiously and destructively.

Evidence of post-war survivors feeling guilty at surviving is almost purely anecdotal. Perhaps they were good at keeping it to themselves or could find no way of expressing it. Those who escaped the horrors of the trenches may have suffered other forms of guilt.

In John Masters' novel of the First World War 'By the Green of the Spring,' one of the characters, when asked if he would be willing to support an initiative set up to help disabled ex-servicemen, says "You've hit a spark. I was feeling guilty... I personally had a jolly interesting war. We took Jerusalem, so now we can really say, 'Next year in Jerusalem.' The Bank made millions out of the war. Oh we earned it, but nevertheless we made a lot of money... And I at least haven't slept too well since, thinking of those who didn't have such a good time.

...So I'm with you all the way."

"It'll cost you a lot."

"Not as much as two legs, two eyes, or a sound mind."

A sense of loss

Many people lost many things in the "Great War". Some lost everything and more. *"This is the story of Elizabeth Cranston and her family. Seven of her sons enlisted to fight in the First World War. Four were killed, two were severely wounded and their youngest brother bore the scars of guilt and heartbreak for the rest of his life.*

Worst affected of the survivors was Elizabeth, whose world understandably fell apart when her sons failed to return from the battlefields of France and Belgium or came home maimed and broken. The first was James, a stonemason, who joined the Royal Engineers. He didn't even make it to France; he caught TB in Surrey where he was billeted and within 4 months this father of four was dead. A few months later in 1916 his older brother Ian, by now a company sergeant major, was told he would be going home and wrote to his wife of three years to tell her the good news. Two weeks later he was killed at the battle of the Somme.

At this stage Lizzie was beginning to lose her mind. She had postmen handing her death notices, daughters-in-law coming to her weeping. She had grandchildren who had no idea what was going on. And then one week after the death of Ian, William was blown up by a stick grenade. It removed three fingers, badly damaged one of his eyes and covered him in shrapnel wounds. He was a talented violinist and at that moment all possibility of becoming a professional disappeared. At the end of 1916 Adam was killed in his very first action at the battle of Serre, on the Somme.

Lizzie began suffering from obsessive compulsive disorders and started washing dishes endlessly. Two years later her eldest son Alexander was killed during the last offensive of the war, George was 'discharged with thanks' after being wounded three times and mustard-gassed. Each death or injury threw Lizzie further out of kilter.

Only Lizzie's youngest son, Robert, returned from the war unscathed. He arrived home to find devastation all around him, so he moved to join his sister in Australia. There he deteriorated rapidly. He blamed himself for not being able to save his elder brothers and drank himself to death. Sister Mary ended up in a psychiatric institution and George was disabled. William was the only sibling to stay but he suffered from debilitating loneliness.

Lizzie also left for Australia, where she continued to deteriorate, physically and mentally. She wandered through the bush, took all her clothes off and felt drawn to railway stations. Here she would sit for hours waiting for her boys to come home. She died in a mental institution."
Jane Warren

A city at war

For the men from Sheffield there was a particular irony in the militarisation which the war brought. Joining up gleefully from making shells in the steelworks of their hometown to blast the Bosch, they were soon ducking shells directed towards them by the Hun.

And for whom did Harold Beck write his "Song of Sheffield"; the steelworkers? The Steel Barons? The profiteers?

"Shells, Shells, Shells! The song of the city of steel.
Hammer, turn and file, Furnace and lathe and wheel.
Tireless machinery, Man's ingenuity
Making a way for the martial devil's meal.
Shells, Shells, Shells!
Out of the furnace blaze, Roll, Roll, Roll,
Into the workshops maze, Ruthless machinery
Boring externally, Boring a hole

Shells, Shells, Shells! The song of the city of steel
List to the Devil's mirth, Hark to their laughter's peal,
Sheffield's machinery, Crushing humanity
Neath devil-ridden death's impassive heel."

The nature of disablement

The men of Painted Fabrics had many and various physical disabling injuries, officially recorded in chilling detail.
'They said they would never work again'. So proclaimed the headline of the local paper in a feature on Painted Fabrics.
"Corporal Simpson suffered from an amputated right arm and lost half his left hand. He was a butcher before the First World War and as a result of his disability he came

to Painted Fabrics as a broken man, even more in mind than in body. He was unable to dress, wash or feed himself.”

All the men employed at Painted Fabrics were 100 per cent disabled – this meant that they had lost two limbs and were eligible for a full pension, so they could be employed on a part-time basis according to their health and strength. Mental health issues such as fits, seizures, epilepsy and neurasthenia were mentioned almost in passing.

Private John Edward Graydon of the 17th Royal Fusiliers came from Batley in West Yorkshire and was born in 1896, the son of John Graydon, who was a wholesale fruit merchant, and Clara Jane. The family moved to Sheffield and lived at 29 Argyll Street, Meersbrook. John Graydon was apprentice to an engineer turner machinist at a local tool manufacturer when he joined up. He had a younger brother, Richard, and an older sibling, Percy, who was a clerk in a cabinet makers. His left leg was amputated.

Private George Rosewarne was born in 1895 in Chapel Street, Sheffield and lived in Hillsborough, or 'Owlerton' as it was known then, close to the football ground, home of Sheffield Wednesday, the 'Owls'. He was a labourer at the local gasworks at Neepsend. He joined up with the 2nd Yorks and Lancs Regiment on August 21st 1914. His initial training was at Pontefract and he was posted on the 8th November 1915 and discharged on the 13th April 1917. He was wounded in the Dardanelles as part of the Mediterranean Expeditionary Force on the 27th September 1915. He had lost his right hand and suffered gunshot wounds to his left arm, side and leg.

J.W Lanham, from Romford in Essex, joined the Essex Regiment on the 30th of May 1915 and served in France until his discharge on the 3rd of January 1919. He was awarded the Military Medal and came to Painted Fabrics with a part amputated right arm and left hand.

Private Frederick Poules, 30885, of the King's Own Yorkshire Light Infantry, enlisted on the 7th of December 1915 and was discharged on the 11th of October 1918. He was born in 1890 in Sheffield and lived in Aberdeen Street. His father was a compositer/printer and his mother a char. He had a younger brother who was a cardboard box liner. Fred arrived at Painted Fabrics with an amputated left arm and gunshot wounds to both legs and his side, a total of 37 wounds.

Arthur Fisher had both his legs amputated. He balanced on his stumps with the aid of a stick.

William Brookes was 19 years and 11 days old when he joined the Army and was sent to fight in France. He had only been there for 6 weeks when he was hit by a shell which had come over his trench. It took his leg off below the knee. He didn't remember a thing until he woke up in a field hospital where he was surrounded by people speaking French and German. His original wound was below the knee but gangrene had set in so his whole leg had to be removed. William ended up at Painted Fabrics.

The Working Man's Ballet

Disabled

He sat in a wheel chair, waiting for dark.
And shivered in his ghastly suit of grey,
Legless, sewn short at elbow. Through the park.
Voices of play and pleasure after day,
Till gathering sleep had mothered them from him
About this time Town used to swing so gay
When glow lamps budded in the light blue trees.
And girls glanced lovelier as the air grew dim-
In the old times, before he threw away his knees.
Now he will never feel again how slim
Girls waists are, or how warm their subtle hands
All of them touch him like some queer disease.
Now he is old, his back will never brace
He's lost his colour, very far from here,
Poured it down shell holes till the veins ran dry.
And half his lifetime, lapsed in the hot race,
And leap of purple spurted from his thigh.
One time he liked a blood smear down his leg,
After matches carried shoulder high
It was after football, when he'd drunk a peg'.
Germans he scarcely thought of; all their guilt, And Austria's, did not move him.
And no fears of fear came yet.
Some cheered him home, but not as crowds cheer-Goal!
Only a solemn man who brought him fruits
Thanked him; and then enquired about his so
Now he will spend a few sick years in Institutes,
And do what things the rules consider wise,
And take whatever pity they may dole.
Tonight he noticed how the women's eyes
Passed from him to the strong men that were whole.

Wilfred Owen

JEREMY PAXMAN writes:-

"There was one particular type of wound that was particularly distressing to look at. Sentries raising their heads over the parapets to look into no man's land, men advancing into a hail of machine gun bullets, an unlucky hit from a trench mortar, or a fire on a ship or plane, tank or in a trench. Or above all the flying indiscriminate shrapnel from exploding artillery – there were multiple opportunities to acquire some of the worse wounds of all. The dead would later be memorised; the disfigured and maimed lived on. The wife or mother who had waited anxiously for their return blanched when they saw them. Even their own children could not bear to look at them or fled in terror.

Harold Gillies, the surgeon who did more than almost anyone else to have the treatment of disabled soldiers taken seriously, gave some indication of the gravity of the situation when he described the casualties referred to him after the first day of the Battle of the Somme. He had been warned beforehand to expect extra casualties arriving from the first day of the big offensive, anticipating as many as 200. Over 2,000 arrived.

The fighting forced the medical profession to learn fast how to save more lives, and there had been huge advances in battlefield first aid, antiseptics, anaesthetics and orthopaedic surgery – especially the recognition of the importance of 'wound excision', or the cutting away of all dead tissue and the extraction of debris to prevent gangrene. Military surgeons tried to patch up the injured by sewing the sides of a wound together, leaving a shorter or narrower limb.

Remember Me

The establishment of many institutions and facilities to help those in need after the end of the war were started with a strong association with memorials to the 'fallen' of the war. One such establishment was Toc H (Talbot House), established by the Rev. P.B (Tubby) Clayton, in memory of his friend Gilbert Talbot, a subaltern who was killed leading his men in an attack near Hooge in Belgium.

A small Plaque is set in the wall of the Territorial Army Barracks on West Street, Sheffield. It's in full view of tens of thousands of Sheffield citizens who go backwards and forwards each day to work and play on foot or bike, by bus, tram and car, but it remains unseen by all but a few.

The Plaque, similar to countless others in Flanders, Britain and its Colonies, reads:-

TO THE GLORY OF GOD

AND IN HONOURED MEMORY OF THE

OFFICERS, NON-COMMISSIONED OFFICERS AND

MEN OF THE WEST RIDING DIVISIONAL

ROYAL ENGINEERS WHO GAVE THEIR LIVES

FOR KING AND COUNTRY IN THE GREAT WAR.

1914-1918

I have not gone away, if you remember me

Demobilisation after the end of the war in 1918 was often painfully slow. The demobilisation systems could be very unfair, to the extent that there was serious talk of mutiny at Calais and Étaples. As a result, some of the stronger real feelings of soldiers towards their superior officers were vented. Again in John Masters 'By the Green of the Spring', dated Flanders January 1919, the following ugly incident takes place:-

"He held up the paper to the light and cried 'This is a message to all of you from Field-Marshall Douglas Haig, Commander-in-Chief of the British Expeditionary Force.' The man who had been speaking beforehand shouted, "Shut up! We aren't listening to anything Haig has to say to us." Gregory raised his voice and continued, "Your action in refusing to obey orders…"

The soldier shouted, "Sing, mates, Sing, Let's give 'em the Red Flag!" He waved his hand in time. They were yelling at the tops of their voices, Gregory yelling back at them. A soldier who had broken away from the rest of the group muttered in his ear, "Better go, Sir, You've done your best." Gregory saw that the man was from his own corps and said, "What are you doing with these scum, you're a Sapper!" "No use arguing now Sir. The Bolshies are in charge and no one's going to fight them 'cos we're all fed up, including me!"

A sting in the tail

In the months that led up to the November 11th Armistice of 1918 the armies and navies of the world had begun to disperse. On their way home the demobilised survivors took with them a deadly virus. The fetid, rat-infested trenches provided ideal breeding grounds for the virus that would be responsible for more than five times the number of deaths worldwide than the war itself. The virus was thought to have originated in chickens and mutated in pigs before emerging in humans in the spring of 1918.

In the autumn the nation was struggling to come to terms with the catastrophe of the First World War. Nearly three quarters of a million British men were estimated to have died and a million and a half were severely wounded during the conflict. Almost no surviving individual escaped the grief of losing a husband, father, son, fiancé, uncle, cousin or friend.

Those afflicted by the so-called 'Spanish' flu were first aware of a shivery twinge at breakfast. By lunchtime, their skin had turned a vivid purple. By the evening death would probably have occurred, often caused by choking on the thick scarlet jelly clogging their lungs. 15 to 40 year olds were most susceptible. Those who had survived the war had little or no immunity acquired during previous flu epidemics by members of older generations.

The chance of passing on the disease increased with the gathering of huge Armistice crowds and the understandable close contact of reunited families and couples.

At the beginning of the outbreak the Royal College of Physicians announced that this strain of flu was not a serious threat. The Times newspaper even suggested that the swift spread of the epidemic might have been a direct result of "the general weakness of nerve power known as war-weariness." Poet T. S. Eliot concluded after the war that "humankind cannot bear that much reality."

The General Medical Council discouraged use of the word pandemic and news of the outbreak was buried deep within newspapers. But the escalating death rate could not be ignored, swelling the increasing fear of the disease. Drastic measures were taken as the worldwide spread of the flu could not be contained. Handshaking was outlawed in certain parts of the USA and in France spitting became a legal offence. People went about their business with noses and mouths bandaged and scarved against catching the infection. A small gauze mask made from three layers of butter muslin and worn across the mouth and nose seemed to inhibit the virus.

The authorities struggled to cope as the epidemic took hold. In London nearly 1,500 policemen, a third of the force, reported sick simultaneously. Council office workers took off their suits and ties to dig graves. Coffins that had been stockpiled during the war (due to a wartime agreement that no bodies would be brought back from the battle lines) were suddenly in short supply. Railway workshops turned to coffin manufacturing and Red Cross ambulances became hearses.

Whole classes of children were kept away from school by their terrified parents. The children sang the rhyme:-

I had a little bird
Its name was Enza,
I opened the window
And in flew Enza.

The flu epidemic began to prey on people's already fragile minds and there were suicides by those who could not cope with yet another struggle for survival after the long debilitating experiences of the war. Worn out by the conflict they thought would never end and with all fledgling hope for a happier future destroyed by threat of the flu's onset, they succumbed.

Buses were sprayed with disinfectant and Councils insisted public places should be emptied every four hours to allow windows to be opened to aerate halls.

Medical advice as to how avoid the flu was scant. Most doctors and nurses were attending to war casualties, overwhelmed by the numbers. And they too were not immune to the flu.

The epidemic was over by the end of 1919 but not before an estimated 228,000 civilians had died in Britain alone.

Duty of care

By the Green of the Spring

Guy spoke slowly and carefully. He said:-

"There are four organisations trying to look after ex-servicemen… see that they get their disability pensions… help them find jobs… create jobs even. I know that Field-Marshall Haig is very concerned about all that, and will take too active part when he retires. What we want to do is something more ambitious.

We want to take these wrecks… These people which the War crushed under its tracks, and if we can make them more than they were before. We think that there is music in the souls of many men who have never had the chance to let it grow, flourish, take over. Art, even… the whole horizons of art, and all its nooks and crannies, and give them what skills they will need – and have the capacity to absorb?

Why should such people not formulate ideas about the way in which we should reorganise the world, using what we have learned in the war, studying the changes that have come about, and the reasons for them?"

"How are you going to set about it?"

"Get an estate, with a big house, with room to build more… or put up Nissen huts… then take in the wounded, the sick. Find teachers. Knock down barriers. Build roads back to ability, pride, and beyond."

"You'll have resident staff then?"

"Enough, but we'll have to be near some big city, so that local doctors, dentists, specialists and experts of all kinds can make a contribution without having to travel great distances."

John Masters

Après La Guerre was a soldier's song sung to the tune of 'Under the bridges of Paris':
"Après la Guerre finis,
Soldat Anglais partis;
Mam'selle Fran say boko pleuray,
Mademoiselle in the family way,
Après la guerre finis."

The gay prospect of a post-war homecoming soon became stark reality for the traumatised troops to face. Rifleman Fred White, 10th Battalion, and King's Royal Rifle Corps, said:

"It took us years to get over it. Years! Long after when you were working, married and had kids, you'd be lying in bed with your missus and you'd see it all before you. Couldn't sleep, couldn't lie still. Many and many is the time when I've got up and tramped the streets till it became daylight. Walking, walking, anything to get away from your thoughts. And many are the times I've met another chap that was out there doing exactly the same thing. That went on for years."

Survivors not wanted

Vera Brittain served as an auxiliary nurse during the war and tragically lost many of her talented and creative friends. She never recovered but later compiled a personal narrative and thoughtful and incisive analysis of the war and its impact. She particularly brought together a deeper analysis and overview of not only what happened to her and her friends but also how it affected everyone in society. In her account of the post-war nation, 'Testament of Youth,' she writes:-

"Why couldn't I have died in the War with the others?" I lamented. Why couldn't a torpedo have finished me, or an aerial bomb, or a zeppelin raid, a mortar shell, a buzz bomb, a machine gun bullet, or gas, or one of those annoying illnesses? I'm nothing but a piece of wartime human wreckage, living ingloriously in a world that doesn't want me."

"Obviously it wasn't a popular thing to have been close to the war. Patriots, especially of the female variety, were as much discredited in 1919 as they had been honoured in 1914."

"No doubt the post-war generation was wise in its assumption that patriotism 'had nothing to do with it' and we pre-war lot were just poor boobs for letting ourselves be kidded into thinking it had."

Her poem 'The Lament of the Demobilised' vividly puts over these views:

"Four years, some say, consolingly. 'Oh well,
What's that? You're young. And then it must have been,
A very fine experience for you!'
And they forget How others stayed behind and just got on -

Got on the better since we were away.
And we came home and found,
They had achieved and men revered their names,
But never mentioned ours;
And no one talked heroics now, and we must go back and start again once more.
You threw three or four years into the melting pot —
'Did you indeed!' these others cry, 'Oh well,
The more fool you!'
And we are beginning to agree with them.

She later said:

"Today, as I look back, 1919 seems a horrid year, dominated by a thoroughly nasty peace.
It appeared to an exhausted world as divine normality, the spring of life after the winter of death,
the stepping stone to a new era, and the gateway to an infinite future — one in whose promise
we had to believe, since it was all some of us had left to believe in."
Condemned to live in a world without security or confidence, a world in which every dear
personal relationship would be tearfully cherished under the shadow of apprehension; in which
love would seem perpetually by death and happiness appear a house without duration.
 Built upon the shifting sands of chance."

The Women to the Men Returned

"You cannot speak to us nor do we reply:
You learnt a different language, where men die,
Are mutilated, maddened, blinded, torn
To tatters of red flesh, mown down like corn'
Crucified, starved, tormented. Oh forgive
Us, who whilst all men died could bear to live
Happy, almost, excited, glad, almost,
Extravagantly, counting not the cost —
The cost you paid in silence. Now speech is vain,
We cannot understand nor do you explain

Your passion and your anguish; we are deaf
And blind to all except customary grief,
How shall our foolish consolations reach
Trouble that lies so deeper far than speech?
Your secret thought – what is it? We do not know;
Never such gulf divorced you from the foe
As now divides us, for how may you tell
What Hell is to us who only read of Hell."

Margaret Sackville

News from nowhere

*"Alone and shivering on the pavement, he thought about taking a taxi and decided against it.
The walk would do him good, and if he hurried he could probably make it back in time. Now
Roberts had gone he hated everybody: giggling girls, portly middle-aged men, women whose eyes
settled on his wound stripe like flies. Only the young soldier, home on leave, staggering out of
the pub, dazed and vacant-eyed, escaped his disgust."*

*"After a few days of safety, all the clear spirit of the trenches was gone. It was still, after all these
weeks, pure joy to go to bed in white sheets and know that he would wake. The road smelled
of hot tar, moths flickered between the trees, and when at last turning up the drive he stopped
and threw back his head, the stars burst on his upturned face like spray."*

*"When it was over, you know what we got? A kick up the backside by the government. The
unemployed soldier had a hell of a time until the order came through that anyone employing
an ex-serviceman could not sack him."*

"They never gave me any allowance for the effects of the gas."

Personal column, The Times 1919

"Old Etonian [27], married and suffering from neurasthenia but in no way really incapacitated, in need of outdoor work.
Would be glad to accept post of head gamekeeper at nominal salary."

Vera Koenig, Headcorn, Kent, The Independent 2014

"I was saddened to read the article about Edward Thomas [2nd June]. My father too went off to the First World War leaving a sick wife and two malnourished children. He came home a broken man in mind and body – being gassed so badly that he died when I was three. My mother died when I was nine."
"The war was not glorious, nor were the dead glorious. There were just ongoing, broken lives.
"After the War was over, men were either dead, disabled or survivors. All needed help."

As portrayed in D.H. Lawrence's Lady Chatterley's Lover, the Lady's upper class husband is a war–wounded impotent wreck.

The Soul of a Survivor

If We Return

If we return will England be
Just England still you and me?
The place where we must earn our bread?
We, who have walked among the dead,
And watched the smile of agony.
And seen the price of liberty,
Which we have taken carelessly
Dread lest we should hold blood guiltily
From other hands. Nay we shall dread.
If we return
The things that men have died to free.

F.W. Harvey

I Want To Go Home – A Soldier's Song

I want to go home
I want to go home
I don't want to go in the trenches anymore
Where the wiz-bangs and the shrapnel they whistle and they roar
Take me over the sea
Where the Alley man can't get at me
Oh my I don't want to die
I want to go home, I want to go home, I want to go home
I don't want to visit La Belle France no more
Oh the Jack Johnsons they make such a roar
Take me over the sea, Where snipers they can't get at me
Oh my, I don't want to die, I want to go home

They

The Bishop tells us: 'When the boys come back
They will not be the same for they will have fought
In a just cause; they lead the attack
On Anti-Christ; their comrade's blood has bought
New right to breed an honourable race.
They've challenged death and dared him face to face
'We're none of us the sae!' the boys reply
For George has lost both his legs; and Bill's stone blind;
Poor Jim's shot through the lungs and like to die;
And Bert's gone syphilitic; you'll not find
A chap that served who hasn't found some change.
And the Bishop said, 'The ways of God are strange!'

Siegfried Sassoon

Aftermath

Do you remember the hour of din before the attack?
And the anger, the blind compassion that shook you then?
As you peered at the doomed and haggard faces of your men?
Masks of the lads who once were keen and kind and gay?
Have you forgotten yet?
Look up and swear by the green of spring that you will never forget.

Siegfried Sassoon

A land fit for heroes

Robin Burden writes:

"*Soldiers returning from WWI were initially greeted with gratitude and respect from their respective nations. However the years that followed were difficult for a number of veterans for a number of reasons. When soldiers returned from the front, they were greeted with a hero's welcome. Parades and flag-waving were the order of the day.*

However most soldiers only received a few weeks' wages after they came back from the war, and a couple of medals. They were then expected to get back to their pre-war routines. Needless to say this was almost impossible.

Social attitudes towards returning war heroes were also fairly complicated. Whilst no-one doubted the bravery of the soldiers who made it back, the nation's mourning for those who didn't caused problems for those who survived.

Because the war dead were revered so much people often spoke of 'the nation's best men being lost to war'. This understandable attitude implied that those who did manage to return were somehow less important or less brave than their fallen comrades.

Unfortunately for the returners, who would have liked nothing more than to completely forget, mourning nations seemed rightly obsessed with reliving and 'honouring' the past, especially, and to some extent exclusively if they had died. Most WWI war memorials to this day admonish us 'Lest We Forget.'

There were also political pressures. Whilst WWI was seen as the 'War to end all wars', the seeds

102

of WWII had already been sown and the mere thought of this must have horrified men who were in any way involved in WWI."

Euphoria at the end of the war

Everyone Sang

Everyone suddenly burst out singing;
And I was filled with such delight
As prisoned birds must find in freedom,
Winging wildly across the white
Orchards and dark-green fields; on - on - and out of sight.

Everyone's voice was suddenly lifted;
And beauty came like the setting sun:
My heart was shaken with tears; and horror
Drifted away ... O, but Everyone
Was a bird; and the song was wordless; the singing will never be done.

Siegfried Sassoon

This celebratory poem was set to music and included as a test piece at the International Eisteddfod at Llangollen, North Wales, almost 100 years later by the local Bolsterstone Male Voice Choir.

Back home

For many the euphoria of the victory marching and communal singing did not last long. Soldiers were often ignored on their return, while others were ostracised and exploited – often those who had been wounded and were least able to look after themselves.

Gunner William Towers, Royal Field Artillery:
"I got involved working with BLESMA – the British Limbless Ex-Servicemen's Association. We all got to know all the limbless men and where they lived – and somehow we circulated the news among them when there was any form of gathering.
"A fellow called Cyril Stevens stood up and started the meeting, "First of all, Gentlemen, welcome. The first thing you need to do is to propose someone as chairman.
"We were having a lot of trouble with the people who fitted the limbs in those days – they were fitting us with cheap legs and getting away with it. Some bright spark proposed a Mr Holden as chairman, but this was the funny part: he was the fitter of cheap legs in Chapel Allerton. His "Yes man" was proposed as Secretary.
"There was a company called Desentre making a really beautiful leg but these were fitting cheap ones.

"Generally you would need to replace your leg every 5 or 6 years. I had a new leg but it wasn't the right shape for me. They made fitted legs to a standard shape. But not all men matched the standard. It was nipping my leg every time I walked and caused abscesses. Surgery in hospital was required to remove them. All five wards of the hospital were full and quite a few of the patients had the same troubles as me."

Good to be alive

He came into the crowded village hall and looked round, as if he were searching for something. He was: he was investigating his family history, especially what a paternal grandfather had done in the First World War. There were some scattered bits of information gleaned from some remaining family members, some old papers family members had kept and bits of general information from a visit to the National Archives.

From all this digging it was clear that Albert Edward Leary had joined up as an ordinary Private and remained solidly so until he was discharged in 1919. The chap at the National Archives said that three quarters of the records of WWI soldiers had been destroyed by the Luftwaffe in an incendiary raid on the warehouse where they were kept in Southwark, London, including Albert's. Typical!

The Local History WWI Society had made a special study of local soldier's records and they had a stall at the local Family History Fair in the village hall. The long search was almost over. Surely they would know what grandad Albert Edward of the Kings Own Yorkshire Light Infantry had got up to during the war?

They were all very friendly, bursting with facts, photographs and information, computers and record books at the ready.

"Oh, I'm sure we will be able to help you," the lady said.

"When was it that he died?"

"He didn't," came the grandson's reply, "He was alive at the end of the war and lived until 1934 as a matter of fact."

"Oh but I'm very sorry," she said, "But we have no records of those who survived, only those who died."

So much for the survivors; they quickly became the Army we would prefer to forget. Despite all the talk of 'A land fit for heroes to live in' it was back to the same as when they left for the war for most surviving soldiers: unemployment, overcrowding, illness and poverty – and much worse for many.

They had set off for the battle in the frenzied patriotism of the war fever, gripped by the enthusiasm of a nation and spurred on by a recently-established but powerful national publicity machine, only to return largely unheralded, unsung and unfortunate.

Meet the survivors of Painted Fabrics

In a Soldier's Hospital
Crippled for life at seventeen
His great eyes seemed to Question why,
With both legs smashed it have been
Better in that grim trench to die
Than drag maimed years out helplessly

Eva Dobell

Taffy Llewellyn was one of the men who received rehabilitation, housing and work after WWI at Painted Fabrics, his lower leg amputated and suffering from gunshot wounds to his thigh. Taffy held the most war decorations of the men at Painted Fabrics, including the Military Medal, D.C.M. and Croix de Guerre.

"Men who suffered not only horrific injuries including amputations but the subsequent psychological effects. One man in particular, who had lost both his right hand and his left hand and forearm, was in a state of hopeless despair."

Most had suffered amputations of arms and legs, or both. Some also had neurasthenia or gunshot wounds. The scale of their disablement can be gauged from the distressing statistic given in one publicity leaflet…

"47 men with only 56 undamaged arms and 50 undamaged legs between them."

"Another man was out in France during the War and his greatest pal was mortally wounded. He turned to our man and said, 'George, when it's all over and you get back, will you marry Lucy'? Lucy was the wounded man's wife.

"Anyhow, George did marry Lucy, who brought three children with her. By this time our man had lost both his legs and received a full pension of two guineas a week. He could get no work and rented one room for which he paid eighteen shillings and six pence per week.

"We arranged to take him and when he arrived he was greeted with, 'where are your things'? He said, 'Oh my Wife's got them'. She had a small parcel in her hands, and contained in that parcel was a quilt. That was the sum total of the whole of their possessions.

"An immediate visit was paid to one of the salesrooms in Sheffield and goods were purchased (we have a fund which is used for such cases), and the man's house, to some extent, was furnished.

"That man today has a perpetual smile. He says that life is wonderful and well worth living."

Annie Bindon Carter did not miss any opportunity to express her pride and affection for the men and staff of Painted Fabrics.

Visits often included a tour of the site, and her carefully-prepared notes indicate how each department and each person were of the utmost importance in the telling of the Painted Fabrics story, especially to Royal visitors who could no doubt do them a great deal of good.

Passages taken from Annie Bindon Carter's notes for Royal visits in 1929 include:-

"FIRST THE NAMES OF THE MEN WORKING IN THE DIFFERENT DEPARTMENTS OF PAINTED FABRICS AND THEIR TIME OF SERVICE AT TIME OF ROYAL VISIT , INDICATING THEIR YEARS OF SERVICE:-

CLUB ROOM, Steward-B. Ellis-4

STENCIL ROOM, H. Gregory-8, R.A Grindel-4.5, H. Hammerton-2.5, J. Bull-1.25.

MAIN WORKSHOP, Foreman-H. Simpson-8.5, A.Hardy-10, W. Thackery-8,.A. Wildgoose-10,.G. Rosewarne-10, W. Whitham-10, G. Goode-10, F. Poules-10, T.W. Llewellyn-5.5, E. Shooter-10, H. A. Riley-5.5, W. Walker-4.5, B. Callaghan-4.5, A. Johnson-4.5, R. A. Grindel-4, C.N. Wiggins-4.5, H. Bownes-4, A. Loxley-4. J. Murray-3, A. Harper-2.5, H. Hems-2.5, J.J. Lawless-1.25

LEATHER DEPARTMENT, Foreman C. Marlow - 3, G.A. Cooper - 1.5, A.J. Sutton - 2.5, Green -.25

OFFICES, S.A. Cooks - 8.5, D.J. Rees-3, J.E. Gragon-1.5, T.W. Wilson -.25

STOCK ROOM, A.J. Cole-8, C. Brittain - 3

MAKING UP DEPARTMENT, A.G. Hartland - 4.

SASMA ROOM, Foreman-R.H. Vernon-9, A.Rhodes-3, W.C. Brookes-4, F. Donahoe-2, J. Fox-2, F. Dean-2, B. Roe-1.5, Montgomery-1.5, Ashworth-.2, 5Easto-.25."

"These most masculine of men producing the most delicate, decorative of feminine products for the ladies of the land.

"The first cottage inspected will be occupied by a man named Cpl. Rees who was shortly to be married. The house was furnished out of his own savings since working with Painted Fabrics.

"Along the corridor to the Club and here if wet the Painted Fabrics Brownie pack will be, but if fine, they will be in the open space between the club and the stencil room.

"Next comes the stencil room where five men are working on the making, repairing, cleaning and cataloguing of 1,600 stencil plates."

Works Manager Cpl. H. Simpson [amputation right arm and half left hand, remainder useless.] "This man is one of the most wonderful Printed Fabrics have come across. A butcher before the War – as result of his disability he came to Printed Fabrics entirely broken, even more in mind than in body – but notwithstanding the fact he is unable to dress, wash or feed himself he is entirely responsible for the giving out of work to all the men, cataloguing all designs, training new men and in every sense a capable Works Manager. By means of special brushes he can stencil and teach others to do so. We are very proud of him.

"Through to the main workshop where the majority of the old, original Printed Fabrics men are working, many of them being with us for more than ten years.

"In this room the majority are 100 per cent disablement but in spite of this they are a cheery crew – often singing their old army songs as they work.

"Hardy [amputation of right arm and left leg] commenced work in hospital in 1916 and has worked at Printed Fabrics since then. He was in one of the first boatloads at the Gallipoli landings, where he lost an arm and a leg. He has suffered much domestic trouble also – but notwithstanding this we have not had one bit of trouble with him and he is one of the cleverest workers.

"Another man with wonderful grit and determination, fighting against the odds, is W. Whitham [gunshot wound in head, permanent paralysis left side, fits]. He is 100 per cent disablement and has done over ten years' service with Painted Fabrics.

"The Foreman of the Leather Department is C. Marlow [amputation of left arm].

"Next, inspection of offices where four disabled men are involved then through to the Stock Room where a display of new season's samples were shown. One man is employed on the sewing machine, another one in cutting out. The man at the machine is C. Brittain [amputation of legs from knees], who came to us from Liverpool, where he and his wife and five children had been living in one little attic. In this department are two widowed ladies, mother and daughter, who, for very small salaries to supplement their tiny incomes devote all of their time to Printed Fabrics. Another widow drives the van which collects the men from their homes and collects them at night.

"Next an inspection of the Making-Up room, where one man is employed at a sewing machine and a certain number of the man's daughters are employed in making up. As the younger daughters of the man, they will also be taken into this workshop.

"Mr. A. G. Hartland [gunshot wounds to spine, paralysis] is an interesting case. He came to us from Cheltenham Hospital which was closing down. Hartland was meant to be sent to Roehampton, however it was decided he should be allowed to marry his fiancée who had stuck with him since before the War. The young woman was taken into hospital for some months in order to be able to look after him. They now have a bungalow in the Painted Fabrics estate and are very comfortable and happy".

"The machines these men work on are specially constructed to suit their disabilities.

"From the Making-Up Room across the open space into the SASMA [Soldiers and Sailors Mutual Association] Room to inspect the new machinery which finds employment at the present time for eleven men, and where we hope to take on several more before long. Goods printed in this room are principally manufacturers' own materials.

"The Foreman of the SASMA Room is Mr R. H. Vernon [gunshot wound left arm]. This man had no knowledge of the printing of fabrics before he came to us. He is an intensely interested and capable man."

"There are three widows working at Painted Fabrics…

"Firstly, Mrs White who for many years had sole charge of the stock and received only a very small sum of 30 shillings a week and her own private income, amounted to only a few shillings a week. At one difficult time she worked for no income at all, and has steadfastly refused to have it repaid. Mrs White is now in charge of one of our shops and receives a salary of two pounds and six shillings a week plus commission on sales.

Mrs White's daughter, Mrs Haswell, who is also a widow, has worked continuously for Printed Fabrics getting off stock to all the various exhibitions and orders. She has charge of four disabled men who are particularly difficult cases, being very nervy and one of them has a very serious head wound. She seems to have no time limit and is often working right up to Saturday night. Her wages are two pounds per week. These two ladies are not of the working classes, and for you to be able to judge the type of women, I would point out that Mrs Haswell's hobby is studying foreign languages.

Mrs Marshall worked tirelessly during the war when Painted Fabrics was in the hospitals. About two years ago her husband died very suddenly and left her with little more than one or two shillings a week and a small house. She is a woman of 57 years of age. She applied to me for work and I was unable to offer her anything but driving the van, and though she had not driven a van before she immediately learnt and took on this word, which means going out in all weathers and doing a variety of work from driving men to hospital, bringing them to work and returning at night, matching materials and all the other odds and ends that are required of a van on an estate of this kind. And for you to further appreciate what kind of woman she is can I also tell you that she was also amateur tennis champion of Nottinghamshire."

Hospital Sanctuary

When you have lost your all in a world's upheaval,
Suffered and prayed and found your prayers were vain
When love is dead, and hope has no renewal,
These need you still, come back to them again.

Vera Brittain

Hand written on a small, torn piece of card by a worker at Painted Fabrics.
LOOK AT ME
AM I NO USE?
I THOUGHT SO TILL I MET MRS CARTER.
I AM NOW AS USEFUL AS A WHOLE MAN AND TO SHEW
MY INDEPENDENCE I CAN SMOKE IN HER HOME

A PRESENT TO MRS CARTER, FROM,
THE BOURNEMOUTH DISABLED SAILORS AND SOLDIERS
WORKSHOPS, 228 WIMBORNE ROAD, BOURNEMOUTH,
with the note:-

"FROM THE 'SMILERS', WHO HAD THE GOOD LUCK TO MEET A LADY
LIKE YOU"

"He's a cheery old card," muttered Harry to Jack,
As they slogged up to Arras with rifle and pack.
But he did for them both with his plan of attack."

THE STAR, SHEFFIELD in 1919 reported what was to be considered one of Field Marshall Haig's most calculating and revealing final orders. After the German Army made what was to be their final advance before the end of the war Field Marshall Douglas Haig issued the following order:-

"Backs to the wall. Every man will stand and fight and fall. There will be no more retreating. And believing in the justice of our cause, each one must fight to the end. The safety of our homes and the freedom of mankind alike depend on the conduct of each one of us at this critical moment."

Many took this to mean yet further futile sacrifice of lives and what they thought was appropriate opprobrium followed. This accusation would no doubt have followed Haig through the doors of Painted Fabrics although it is likely that no-one was impolite enough to suggest such a thing outright, and in any case it was clear that 'nobility' would have a significant role as rescuers of the victims of war shortly after being labelled persecutors. Such are the conflicts of interest and dilemmas which businesses of all kinds have to face and work through, and now Painted Fabrics was about to become a proper business.

When the War was finally over, there were still few questioning voices of the total domination of the 'King and Country' mantra, but some, like A.E Houseman, expressed his concerns through his poetry, with the pithy comment:-

No more winters biting,
Filth in trench from fall to spring
Summers full of sweat and fighting,
For the Kaiser or the King
Rest you charger, rust you, bridle. Kings and Kaisers keep your pay!

On side

One of the publicity pictures of Painted Fabrics, taken about 1920, poignantly shows an old man with a trim military moustache posing with the workers on a factory visit connected to the Douglas Haig Homes project. It was Earl Haig himself, former Commander in Chief of the British forces in WWI. In another scene from Painted Fabrics his framed picture is seen hanging on the wall behind the working men.

"Yet without some of his controversial frontline decisions, Painted Fabrics might never have started. Or have been necessary," dryly commented one of the history makers of the day. For some the mere thought that the 'Noblesse' cited here could possibly be classified as 'Perpetrators' in the conflict would be out of the question, but others considered that they at the very least had 'a lot to answer for.'

On the other hand there were definite signs of a more redeeming quality and a welcome generosity of spirit to match the ones which characterised Painted Fabrics. A short time before the late Field Marshall Earl Haig's death a lady left him £1,200 to be used as he thought fit for the benefit of disabled soldiers and sailors. He gave £600 to The British Legion and the same amount to Painted Fabrics.

Class warfare

The issue of "class" of relationship between the classes was generally in the background during the war, although some of the experiences of serving men were commented on in vitriolic terms, showing it had not gone away.

"The only thing that really gets me angry is when people at home say there are no class distinctions at the front. Bollocks! What you wear, what you eat, where you sleep, what you carry. The men are no more than pack animals.

"But you know the worst thing? I used to go to this café in Amiens and just across the road there was a brothel. The men used to queue out onto the street, they got 2 minutes. Officers probably didn't pay! And no doubt went round the back entrance!"

"For you our battles shine,
With triumph half divine;
And glory of the dead,
Kindles in each proud eye.
But a curse is in my head,
That shall not be unsaid,
And the wounds in my heart are red,
For I have watched them die."

What the common soldier perhaps could not quite understand was how the 'higher-ups' could hide their inner thoughts and feelings behind a barrier of orders, reports and strict obedience. Were not they, as fellow human beings, 'brothers in arms', comrades, similarly moved and affected by what was happening? How could they then hide it or clothe it in such distanced, inhuman and lifeless tones? Obviously it was not conducive to military discipline. Even at Painted Fabrics when the horrific consequences of war were there for all to see there was still a strong element of reserve, stoic forbearance and outward politeness and deference.

The road less travelled

Victims of conflict, such as our citizen soldier survivors of the war, have little or nothing to redeem, save for perhaps a perceived but undeserved sense of guilt. The rescuers of conflict, whose story is also told here, may have no personal or collective part to play in the conflict or its redemption, save for a compelling desire and motivation to redeem the after-conflict situation.

The perpetrators of conflict, who may ostensibly have much to be redeemed, may regard the whole process of conflict as irrelevant to them, impossible or completely extraneous. In some senses they are correct – we cannot alter the past – but we can change and transform our relationship to it. We can go back and say the things we did not say, do the things we did not do, directly or through the actions of others.

We can also help to redeem the situation, as was desperately needed at the end of the war.

This path is open to all perpetrators, and was opened up and taken by those in WWI who had responsibility, through the efforts of Annie Bindon Carter and her colleagues, and Painted Fabrics. Many who would qualify under the 'title' noblesse were involved with Painted Fabrics from the beginning.

Annie Bindon Carter unashamedly and unapologetically used her personal influence and example to enlist the support of the Establishment to play their part in her redemptive process. She helped, perhaps inadvertently, to open up a new chapter in their story even after the book had apparently been closed shut after the war.

In John Master's In the Green of Spring on Sunday October 13th 1918, a similar ambition is expressed as one of the characters says:

"It'll be good publicity for me to have the Countess of Swanwick as area manager, especially in London.

"He thought a long time, staring at her. Haughty, brainy, honest, gutsy. She needed the job and would do it right.

"What was it they said, that meant that? Noblesse Oblige? He'd seen it written out and pronounced it Nobles Oblige."

It's who you know

Painted Fabrics was always well-connected, fully living up to the old saying that 'It's who you know, not what you know that matters'.

First (and last) there was Maud, Lady Milton (1877 -1967), Countess Fitzwilliam, formerly Lady Maud Dundas, daughter of the 1st Marquess of Zetland and commonly referred to as the 'Fairy Godmother' of Painted Fabrics.

Maud was married to William Charles de Meuron, 7th Earl Fitzwilliam (1872-1943), who died of cancer in 1946. Billy Fitzbilly, as he was known colloquially, was not exactly like your run-of-the-mill nobility.

Days before the 1926 General Strike, a union deputation called on Billy Fitzwilliam, the 7th Earl, to say that they did not want to follow the national strike call and walk out. "You must," he told them privately, "or you'll let the others down."

During the strike, and the months-long coal dispute that followed, he fed the miner's 2,500 children and turned the grounds at Wentworth into an amusement park to keep the families entertained, with a £25 prize (more than 4 months' pay) on offer for any cricketer who could break one of his windows from the middle of the lawn. Maud Fitzwilliam, Billy's wife, toured the pit villages in a yellow Rolls-Royce packed with provisions for the poor, including the odd live chicken.

The Fitzwilliams' generosity towards the miners was not motivated by any socialist principles. As Billy saw it, providing the best conditions for his men protected him as well as them.

'Billy Fitz' also made Lord Mayor of Sheffield in 1909.

Maud Fitzwilliam was a close friend and confident of Annie Bindon Carter throughout the history of Painted Fabrics and she was always effusive in her praise at what A.B.C had achieved. She would refer to her as 'Binnie' and sign her letters 'Maud Fitz.'

Annie Bindon Carter would openly describe Painted Fabrics as a combination of 'philanthropy and art' which perhaps reveals some of her deeper thoughts and reservations about the role of the philanthropy, and the deeper motives of the noblesse who were being 'obliging'.

She also referred to this combination as 'snob stuff' and 'sob stuff', which was perhaps even more revealing.

Nevertheless Painted Fabrics would boldly and proudly announce itself on letterheads and official documents as being:

"UNDER THE PATRONAGE OF MAUD, COUNTESS FITZWILLIAM,"
and
"UNDER THE PATRONAGE OF H.R.H. THE PRINCESS ROYAL, VISCOUNTESS LASCELLES"

These Royal connections were especially indispensable to the success of Painted Fabrics, as the Princess Royal's shop girl session illustrates:–

After buying a set of boudoir curtains at the 1932 Claridges Sale she was persuaded to help out. It is reported that:-

"She was painfully shy but she agreed to sell on one of the stalls. We put her on the men's ties stall."

People were only too anxious to buy from her so that they would then be able to say:-

"I bought this from the Princess Royal."

Also involved in supporting Painted Fabrics at various other times was the Prince of Wales (later to become the Duke of Windsor) and The Queen, (later to become the Queen Mother), who bought two dresses for her daughter Elizabeth on one occasion.

The Prince of Wales' appearance at the 1933 Christmas sale in Sheffield was a particularly significant coup for the publicity machine of Painted Fabrics. "One of the first stalls to catch the Prince's eye was the silk handkerchief stall."

Reported the Sheffield Daily Telegraph:-

"His interest in this was naturally an exceptional one, for His Royal Highness was a great purchaser of Painted Fabrics' silk handkerchiefs. During his visit he also picked up one or two

check handbags, purses and diaries to admire. Immediately after he had left the sale there was a rush towards these articles and they were quickly all sold out."

He also visited the Painted Fabrics Estate where the men raised their sticks and crutches in salute to form a guard of honour.

Annie Bindon Carter herself proceeded to become quite a local and national celebrity, however never once did she forget to use this as an opportunity to promote Painted Fabrics and support its employees and their work.

Tickets and invitations came in for Mrs Carter to attend various prestigious functions and occasions:-

"Mrs Carter's tickets have arrived for the Coronation of King George VI and Queen Elizabeth [seating in the grandstand next to Westminster Abbey]."

A commemorative centenary pamphlet for the Royal Warrant Holders Association was issued after her attendance in 1940.

Programmes were sent for the visit of Princess Mary to Sheffield in 1925, and the Cutlers' Feast in Sheffield in 1955 was one of many she attended.

Royal visitors of course made the biggest headline news in the local Sheffield newspapers.

The Star reported:

"The Princess made a thorough inspection of the workshops, talking to all the men, and of the showrooms which were a blaze of colour and beauty. She frequently expressed her amazement at the wonderful work and made several purchases, including one of the 'famous' Painted Fabrics scarves."

"Mr A Hardy, formerly of the Royal Navy, and Mr T. Llewellyn, an ex-sergeant of the Welsh Regiment [who holds the D.C. with two bars, the M.M. with two bars, the Croix de Guerre and a Russian decoration], presented H.R.H. with an ivory georgette shawl with heavy silk fringe, stencilled in dainty Pompadour pattern and made up in their own workshop.

Amongst the disabled who will sell the fabrics, painted at Meadowhead Workrooms, will be the youngest recruit of the Sheffield Association, 23-years-old Cyril Owen who lost both legs when a German tank ran over him during the crossing of the Rhine."

A particularly catching headline was:-

"THE PRINCESS AS A PRINTER"

"Opening a new Block Printing Department, the Princess had all the processes explained to her. Taking up one of the wood blocks she printed a design on one of the pieces of material.

She had expressed her wish to try on a green silk handkerchief printed in a flower pattern in the rich shades of the Orient.

'Very delightful' she commented when shown a child's bedspread pictured in quaint nursery rhymes."

Again in 1951 the local newspapers reported the royal presence at Painted Fabrics:-

THE SHEFFIELD TELEGRAPH - NOVEMBER 7th 1951

'THE QUEEN BUYS MEN'S WORK'

"Articles made by Sheffield war disabled men were amongst purchases made by the Queen yesterday at a London sale of work organised by 15 associations concerned with training men and women severely handicapped by war injuries. The exhibition was at the Lord Robert's Workshops, Brompton Road, Kensington. The Queen bought two silk scarves and a satin bedspread with delicately coloured patterns, hand-painted, all made at Painted Fabrics Ltd., a factory at Meadowhead, for men who had been so seriously injured they could not work in industry. The scarves were designs embodying street cries and included pictures of a muffin man, a town crier and a rat catcher." Until the very end Annie Bindon Carter exploited the relationships she had assiduously cultivated for the benefit. But she never lost her common touch in working alongside the Great and the Good, as illustrated by her tongue in cheek remark that sales in Stately Homes *"offered Mrs Smith a chance of visiting Lady Whatnot in her own home!"*

Perhaps this is as good an indication as we are going to get of the ambivalence inherent in Painted Fabrics reliance on a class of people about as far removed from that of the recipients of their largesse as you could get.

There was always an ambiguous irony in the way that Annie Bindon Carter enlisted the support from the upper classes to support the working class beneficiaries of Painted Fabrics.

Whether she did this deliberately and in a calculated way or through what seemed to her to be a natural and obvious appeal to the hearts and purses of her noble friends and acquaintances and through them to others, eventually reaching the very top, she did with efficiency and achieved some spectacular results. How did she do it?

She meticulously climbed the hierarchy of nobility, from minor local gentry with

Lady Wharncliffe, upwards to Maud, Countess Fitzwilliam of Wentworth Woodhouse, Viscountess Lascelles, Princess Mary, and The Princess Royal. The Queen Mother and finally the Monarch and his consort, The King (and Queen), whom the men of Painted Fabrics had ostensibly fought for in the Great War, all through the female line, of course. Through Annie Bindon Carter's efforts, events around Painted Fabrics became a feature of the social calendar, certainly in the early days.

She built up this impressive monolithic support network of patronage and active involvement in every important aspect of the Painted Fabrics commercial life to try to ensure its survival and success.

Apart from the Lord Mayor and Lady Mayoress, Politicians or local Trade Union leaders were not deemed to be as important for sales as the local business community, which in Sheffield meant the Master and Mistress Cutler, and the Chamber of Commerce. The working class were not often included on Painted Fabric's guest lists, but the employees and their families always were.

So Painted Fabrics became prominently represented at many sales and social gatherings of significance to enhance its reputation and profile at:-

• Coronations
• Royal Warrant Award Ceremonies
• Royal visits
• Exhibitions
• Society Weddings

Painted Fabrics products were prominently displayed or worn in:-

• Stately Homes
• Baronial Halls
• Boudoirs and Bedrooms
• Hallways and Living rooms
• In Cathedrals and Castles
• On Alters and Alcoves
• In Theatres and Palaces

All this boded well for the commercial success the business needed to survive and thrive. Painted Fabrics sales and what we would now no doubt call 'marketing' achievements are therefore by no means diminished by examining them within a complex interplay of forces and influences, taking full advantage of the 'noblesse oblige' position which Annie Bindon Carter had worked so assiduously to establish. Opportunities were created and taken for Painted Fabrics' benefit.

By appointment

Royal warrants were another way in which Painted Fabrics' reputation could be enhanced, and they were given to Mrs Carter on a number of occasions.
"Mrs Annie Bindon Carter, M.B.E to hold the place of Printed and Painted Fabric Maker on behalf of Painted Fabrics Ltd."
A Royal Warrant was also given to Annie Bindon Carter from the Prince of Wales 1936-1938. It grandly announced:-
'This Warrant entitles the holder to use the Prince of Wales Badge of Feathers and Coat of Arms in connection with the business.'
Another Royal Warrant was awarded to Annie Bindon Carter by Queen Elizabeth, consort of King George VI 1938-1952, announcing:-
"This Warrant entitles the holder to use her Majesty's Arms in connection with the business of Painted Fabrics"

Behind the scenes

The Press and public were undoubtedly impressed and enthralled by the spectacle of Painted Fabrics, regaled in its noble and regal connections and patronage.
Only in fledgling socialist circles (and there were plenty of those in Sheffield at the time) would questions start to be asked later about some of the ambivalent positions and contradictions inherent between the public stance and the private practices and persona of these various Earls and Countesses, Lords and Ladies, Viscounts and Viscountesses, Barons and Baronesses, Dames and Sirs, not to say Princes, Princesses, Kings and Queens.
Yet no one at the time dared or thought it possible to raise the issues of Earl Haig's

private thoughts when congratulating the disabled men at Painted Fabrics, no more than any other party who had been responsible for arranging their fate by whatever questionable motive.

The inter-family inheritance disputes which had all but destroyed the Fitzwilliam dynasty were not revealed until Catherine Bailey's book 'Black Diamonds,' subtitled 'The Rise and Fall of a Dynasty,' revealed the astonishing happenings at Wentworth Woodhouse paralleling the times when 'Binnie' and 'Maud Fitz' were working together to promote Painted Fabrics.

The slave-owning credentials of the Princess Royal's Lascelles family, later followed by the appalling injustice of the family's grossly inflated rewards of honours and massively distorted 'compensation' payments made to them when the slave trade was abolished, enabling them to establish themselves in Harwood House and as one of the Royal Family's closest relations, (not to say the aforementioned links and overlap between the Royal Families of Europe, specifically the British and the German, the latter so close you could not put a soldier's cigarette paper between them), were not common knowledge or familiar topics of conversation at this time either.

These significant but relatively unexplored aspects of the Painted Fabrics story add to its fascination and enable us with hindsight of history to place it more accurately within its wider social and political context. This kind of detailed and thorough investigation which would now be expected was not practiced in the times of Painted Fabrics when royalty and nobility were involved. If we knew then what we know now in terms of wider social and political views of the Painted Fabrics story and particularly Annie Bindon Carter's relationships with this layer of society, we would perhaps be even more admiring of the efforts of her and her supporters than we are now. It may have been based on an aspect of the conundrum of 'Noblesse Oblige', but it undoubtedly helped Printed Fabrics achieve what it set out to do.

A stately world of all 'front', superficiality, surface and show, with little or no substance, this fantasy world was reflected to some extent in Painted Fabric designs and presentation, especially the wispy and floaty, rural and stylist, beautiful yet illusive ones which typified the complex but coherent Painted Fabrics style.

The Common People

Contrast this with the world of those Painted Fabrics men who produced these goods for the gentry to admire and surround themselves with. Theirs was a world, a reality, which was almost entirely substantial, urban and ugly.

Life was nasty, brutal and short, followed by the well-documented horrors of the War and the subsequent agony of their brutal injuries and humiliating disability. No style or superficial appearances here, only the grim truth.

Before the war society was in turmoil and a revolutionary fervour was in the air, and on the ground.

After the war came more unrest and turmoil, the main victims again the very 'common man' who had been lauded for their 'sacrifice' during the war. After war had finally ended came the General Strike, the Miners' Strike and the Great Depression, and to top it all, WWII.

Yet somehow, during the time of Painted Fabrics contrasting and even dichotomous worlds fused to produce an integrated whole and a workable, sustained arrangement; a symbiosis of unlikely groups of people, sharing the same destiny. This did not stop people of position and some influences from forcefully expressing reservations about the 'all in it together 'messages of the propaganda machine.

Literature of the time portrayed the relationships between officers and 'men' very differently.

In fiction at least, characters such as the 'toff' Officer Major Tietjens in Ford Madox Ford's Parade's End were constantly getting into trouble with their superiors for looking after the interests of their men, treating them like decent human beings rather than a collective group of 'men' to be demeaned, insulted and abused.

Alfred Taylor, father of writer Doris Lessing, wrote on his experiences of the Great War the following:

'There are a generation of men who lived through the slaughter in the trenches and had a profound contempt for the incompetence of the government'.

One of the most distasteful ways in which our innocent citizen soldier was duped by the authorities was through the official and unofficial propaganda machine.

Those responsible for the overall conduct of the war began with a phoney war – fought on a different battlefield, with different weapons, and with only false pride and meaningless advantage the prize and purpose. On these occasions the 'Noblesse' were only too happy to play their pivotal part.

This kind of undercurrent seemed to play no part in the circumstances and attitudes prevalent at Painted Fabrics.

5

A Moral Necessity

- Painted Fabrics Ltd.

Unique amongst the many worthy and desperately-needed initiatives set up to help the tide of desperate victims of the war, Painted Fabrics from the start set out its stall to form a limited company, a business and a place of work for the men it took on. From its inception Painted Fabrics began to be organised and structured in order to make the most of any opportunities for funding and support that became available and open to them; no doubt Mrs Geoffrey Carter was advised and guided by her businessman husband in this task. These funds were then used to build capacity, train people, create jobs, produce and manufacture, sell, market and promote the 'business'. A committee of sorts was formed and the Soldiers and Sailors Mutual Association was registered and S.A S.M.A, as it became to be known, established, working for the time being under the trading name 'Painted Fabrics', later in 1923 to become Painted Fabrics Limited.

The workforce of Painted Fabrics

It was felt essential, even from the first, that some sort of industry should be started from the small beginnings at Wharncliffe War Hospital. Annie Bindon Carter called it a "moral necessity" that Painted Fabrics should be turned into a business and declared this boldly in her early speeches about the new fledgling organisation. This must have caused quite a stir, especially coming from the tiny newcomer addressing the local captains of industry, representing companies and industries going back centuries in Sheffield, the ancestral home of the cutlery trade and Sheffield Plate, where the inventor Harry Brearley first developed stainless steel, just down the road from the mighty industries and armaments factories of the East End.

What is more, she had the audacity to declare that the particular industry she had in mind to develop at the fledgling Painted Fabrics was high fashion!

The 27th of November 1924, was the date on which Painted Fabrics took on its new corporate identity. It now proudly announced itself as PAINTED FABRICS LTD.

Painted Fabrics is the story of the growth and development of a flourishing, real-life industry out of a simple desire to find congenial occupations for men who were struggling to recover from wounds or struggling with greater obstacles. Annie Carter quickly realised that many would never be robust again and that some light occupation would be all that could ever be expected of them.

Despite these limitations, Annie Carter and all those involved with Painted Fabrics achieved a thriving artistic industry. It grew out of their talent and dedication, giving men who had little or no hope a new pride in themselves and a great sense of accomplishment and achievement in the production of excellent saleable work with which they had been closely associated.

The success of the one case of a man who had lost both his hands being able to stencil on fabric inspired Mrs Carter to develop the idea into a proper business, giving work to men who otherwise would have no hope.

She designed fabrics that the men stencilled and made into small items such as tea cosies and table mats which she could sell to friends. The stencils designed by Mrs Carter were hand cut by the men and they began also to process raw fabrics, bleaching and dyeing them as well as stencilling and making them into a range of luxury items such as dresses, shawls, scarves, wall hangings, furnishing fabrics and even theatrical curtains.

A pioneer organisation

Like most organisations of its type and size in post-war Britain, Painted Fabrics started life tightly clustered around the founding pioneer, in this case Annie Bindon Carter, a single-minded, determined individual with a purpose and a cause outside her personal needs and self-interest.

So called 'Pioneer' organisations, such as Painted Fabrics, invariably started from humble surroundings. They would normally operate with very much the same loose management structure and ways of working as the seemingly boundless energy of the pioneer driving them forward against apparently insurmountable odds and somehow holding things together.

Organisations would often steadfastly withstand any internal and external pressures to make themselves more efficient and better organised as they expanded and became more complex, until the developmental crisis which inevitably overtook them could be resisted no more. No doubt there were suggestions for Painted Fabrics along these lines from Mrs Carter's businessman husband, Geoffrey. Many pioneer organisations went under at this stage, unable to adapt to the need to have separated departments, jobs, roles and functions and the requirement to be more efficient, cut costs and be more business-like.

But Painted Fabrics somehow managed to quickly move out of its 'Pioneer' phase of development with seemingly few difficulties and trauma. There was no inevitability about this. Many, many Pioneer organisations, now and then, are unable to meet the challenges they face when they move out of the initial period of what is sometimes called "furious goodwill" to become a more complex and sophisticated organisation. The Painted Fabrics and B.L.E.S.M.A (the British Limbless Ex-Servicemen's Association) magazine 'The Sasmatian', when publishing its 1932 edition, took great pains to describe the various phases of development it had so far passed through. "In order to explain to our new customers the progress the business has made" it said:-

IN THE BEGINNING

The Disabled Sailors and Soldiers Mutual Association [S.A.S.M.A] was founded in 1919 for the purpose of looking after the interests of disabled sailors and soldiers. In 1923 the founders of the Association decided that if they formed a company in conjunction with the association, ran it on strictly business lines under capable management and produce first-class merchandise to sell in the open market at competitive prices, this would be of far greater permanent benefit to the men than a charitable appeal. At that time the Association were specialising in the production of 'painted fabrics' made up into items and were building up a reputation for this kind of work. It was therefore decided to call this new company Painted Fabrics Ltd.

Painted Fabrics was formed in this way and the first four directors were appointed, but it was laid down in the Articles of Association that they cannot draw any personal benefit whatsoever, and that all profits made are to be used for the further development of the business.

THE NEXT MOVE

"When the company was formed the workshops were in a most unsuitable place and the men had great difficulty getting to work each day. The next move was therefore to establish the S.A.S.M.A estate just outside Sheffield. This was established in 1924".

PROGRESS

"During 1924 the company continued to specialise in the production of painted fabrics but in 1925 it was foreseen that other crafts would have to be introduced if a permanent business was to be built up. The first move was to reorganise a section of the works and train the men in 'leather craft'. This was followed by spray painting with fast dye instead of paints. Since then a further section has been started to develop an ancient printing process originally used by the Egyptians over 2,000 years ago."

FURTHER PROGRESS

"In the early days all textile materials had to be purchased in the finished state ready for the men to decorate but the industry has now developed to such an extent that nearly all materials now used in Sasmatian merchandise are now purchased in the raw state, prepared, dyed and printed by the men themselves which has put the cost of this manipulation into the men's pockets in wages, instead of into the pockets of foreign silk merchants."

Business is business

It had been Annie Bindon Carter's ambition right from the very start, to become a proper limited 'company'; to be to all intents and purposes a free-standing, independent, self-sufficient and hopefully successful business.

She set about this task with the same focused energy and dedication which she had shown in setting up Painted Fabrics.

She was sensible enough to surround herself with willing helpers and expert advisors which must have been enormously supportive, crucial at the early stages of Painted Fabrics development as a business. Once again, in fact, an example of how she was able to combine sensible actions with grim determination and compassionate dedication.

But there were differences in the way the company was constituted and formed from the outset.

True, Annie Bindon Carter began to think about a structure and establishment of some kind – a solid foundation from which to expand and grow. But this would be the means to an end not an end in itself, to help the kind of situation she had first come across in Wharncliffe War Hospital, to somehow help men who had suffered greatly, had often reached rock bottom and needed a practical and useful helping hand not just for a short time but on a continuous and regular basis until they could support themselves and regain their confidence and self-esteem.

Open for business

She realised immediately that this required a funded and supported organisation, independent, well run and self-sufficient, something they all could be proud of, feel they were part of and had played an important role in creating, each and every one of them. Painted Fabrics would be a clear example of what a 'good company' business could look like, an exemplar and an inspiration to others. To achieve this in such a short period of time, overcoming many seemingly insurmountable obstacles, was indeed a tremendous achievement.

Painted Fabrics would become an open community project, a 'family' business and a successful producer of valued and admired high quality goods, with a loyal and satisfied customer base, a well-respected member of the local business community, where there had been a long tradition and history of high quality, stability of employment even through difficult trading conditions, prestige organisations with well-known reputations.

Sheffield's Master Cutler could look out on an impressive vista of household-name companies: Mappin and Webb and Sheffield Plate, Viners, Taylors, Rogers the cutlers, then the massive steel works of Charles Cammell, Firth Brown, Bessemer, Hadfields, T.W. Ward, and later the development of stainless and specialist alloy steels. Manufactories, as they were called, pouring out ton after ton of armaments and armour plate, ingots and forgings, rods and wire made into tools and implements famous around the world.

This was the industrial world in and around Sheffield within which Painted Fabrics intended to establish its reputation and status – in fashion. And they succeeded. Painted Fabrics may not have exactly fitted into the traditional mould of a Sheffield company in terms of size and trade but it did in many other important respects. Mrs Carter was described as "the happiest and simplest of people" and an example of the "fine effects that living for others has on one's own outlook." But when it came to taking care of the business side of Painted Fabrics she was sharp-witted and purposeful. Business and industry may not have been her world but Painted Fabrics was.

She used her deep compassion and understanding of the suffering and struggles of others to good effect in furthering the cause of Painted Fabrics which to her was all about the "men", their rehabilitation and development. Even though she had precious little direct experience of business, manufacturing, engineering, therapeutic methods and theories or clinical treatments, nothing was going to stop her achieving the goals she set for Painted Fabrics and her 'men'. In contributing in this way Painted Fabrics helped to redeem to some small extent the worst effects of the cruelty and inhumanity which had drawn these ordinary men into the cesspit of the War and left them with maimed bodies and tragically damaged souls and spirits. Inspired by this task she was fearless and determined in her efforts to do something about the situation, and stir others into helping her without delay.

She unapologetically used the grim realities of the men's situation to tug at the heartstrings of her audiences as part of her sales pitch, and to enlist the support she needed for her 'magnificent obsession'.

Leading from the Front

Annie Bindon Carter's own particular form of business, she realised, might take some time to take shape. It would have all the required formal essentials of a modern business in the early 1920s. In addition it would also have a structure which suited her own unique and personalised form of management. She was no doubt helped in the task of turning Painted Fabrics into a proper business by her husband Geoffrey Carter, a well-known businessman, Justice of the Peace and Freemason.

The Painted Fabrics business was always a means to an end, to help and support its employees. Creating a viable business never became the end in itself.

She never lost sight of what Painted Fabrics was there for and this, with her own dedication and sense of purpose was probably its greatest strength and stood it in good stead in trying times.

Aims were clear and A.B.C could be forceful, determined and resolute, charming, clever and cunning in turn in the pursuit of her goals, for the sole benefit of those in need.

She could be said to have used every trick in the book, and some which she invented herself. She turned out to be a highly skilful and able manager and leader.

Who's being served?

Painted Fabrics quickly became a working community, where everyone, it seems, felt they were needed and valued. In post-World War One Britain these were not the days of unthinking acceptance of authority and meek, unquestioning obedience at work – too much else had happened for that. These were the days of army mutinies, militant trade union activity and not that much later, a massive national miner's strike and even a General Strike.

Nevertheless it would have been unprecedented if any of this kind of nonsense had spread to a rehabilitation programme for severely disabled ex-service personnel, run by a set of art students in a leafy suburb – even in the hotbed of new socialist ides which was Sheffield.

However even in this tense atmosphere, Painted Fabrics did seem to manage to build a commercial organisation which seemed to have a remarkably philanthropic and even democratic regime, where the 'workers' were peculiarly well respected and cared for. In most other organisations more of a master/servant relationship still prevailed.

Annie Bindon Carter was profoundly affected by the first meeting she had with the severely disabled serviceman she came across in the grounds of Wharncliffe War Hospital in 1917. She felt she had to do something to help men like him, who were in deep despair and had all but given up.

They were the living embodiment of the evils of the war, wandering hopelessly in the community, and they were not going to disappear from the sight and consciences of those who could not turn away and abandon them.

Even with this strong motivation it was difficult, at first, to see what could be done for them, so desperate was their plight. But the reality of these victims of war would not go away.

Some kind of intervention was urgently needed, to provide some kind of refuge, a respite from the agony of their situation, to offer restitution, redemption even, restore some pride, some self-esteem to those whose experiences on others' behalf deserved at least this. She was compelled to try and do something and the nature of her commitment (plus a sparky refusal to give up easily) drove her on.

To offer help in a practical way needed a further leap (not to say a gigantic stride) in imagination, a load of inspiration and some spark of intuition.

Successful businesses and organisations must have a strong sense of purpose. Annie Bindon Carter was clear on what purpose Painted Fabrics Ltd would serve from the very beginning and she never lost sight of it for one moment, right to the end.

Men at work

Mrs Carter often opened her promotional talks to audiences with a challenge…

"Gentlemen," she would say, "I am going to start by asking you two questions.

Firstly have you ever sat in a chair or laid on your bed, and been unable to rise, absolutely tied to the spot?

Have you walked to a door and been unable to open it?

Many of the men employed by Painted Fabrics are in this position".

Mrs Carter claimed the reason for adopting what was often called the 'Luxury Trade', was solely on account of these disabilities. It was a trade where a man could lie, sit or stand. It was the only physical work that a large percentage of the disabilities of the men could do. The 'Luxury Trade' provided unending interest in the production of the various patterns and it was possible for a man without hands and other serious disabilities to be employed.

Others required a variation of light work and we were able to pass these cases through painting, cutting out, packaging and finishing so as making variations in the positions of work, enable a change of working environment and a change of work process. As well as medical, clinical and surgical treatment, the men were provided with other forms of assistance.

From the house and into the single storey workrooms there were a network of covered passages through which men in wheelchairs could drive to their benches. She also verified that:-

"Mental therapy is part of our work. That is why we frequently change round the men's jobs and the constantly changing patterns and colours in the materials worked, preventing boredom."

Annie Carter's efforts and those of her colleagues needed a level of practical application and engineering which was astonishing in its ingenuity and boldness to even attempt to achieve the goals she had set herself. No problem would appear which could not be solved. If solutions did not already exist, they would be found, and possibilities developed to meet the very particular needs and requirements of Painted Fabrics.

Setting a standard

In commercial circumstances where only the very best in terms of product quality, delivery, presentation and sales would do, every effort must be made to establish and maintain the highest standards, with no compromise.

If this was difficult to achieve within the limitations of a severely disabled workforce then these challenges would be faced and overcome. If the level of supervision and management needed to be raised, then this need would be addressed, and attended to. Recruitment would be from the ranks of staff already employed. Painted Fabrics would grow its own.

Painted Fabrics had a style of working which was both benign and philanthropic, based firmly on values and an ethos of service to chosen others on the basis of their need and the ability of others to help, without any element of pecuniary reward, or self-aggrandisement.

Painted Fabrics was different from other pioneer organisations in making an early conscious and planned decision to make itself into a 'proper' business, even more so to become a limited liability company, Painted Fabrics Ltd. Annie Bindon Carter wanted this status for Painted Fabrics and she wanted it quickly, and for sound, thought-through reasons. She wanted Painted Fabrics to become a legitimate business in its hometown and community of work, production and manufactories. She wanted to 'make things', as was the style in Sheffield. More than this she wanted her Painted Fabrics to manufacture things which were attractive and useful. As her unofficial slogan forcefully declared to the world, for Painted Fabrics employees, the whole, unequivocal reason for its existence, she wanted 'work, not charity.'

To carry out legitimate work she needed a business, and a proper one at that, firmly based within the Sheffield business community, where the slogan 'Where's there's muck there's money' meant something to the many independent entrepreneurs who made something of themselves out of nothing and went on to become owners of steel-making empires, steel barons and local dignitaries.

Business-like

Annie Carter herself took extra care to explain why creating a free-standing, independent business was especially important to her and the men she was so committed to helping in this particular way, as a prelude to her many talks and lectures about Printed Fabrics to a wide variety of different audiences.

She was always business-like and precise in her descriptions of Painted Fabrics as a business or 'industry,' especially the jobs it created, the skills and capacities its employees developed, the projects undertaken and the work carried out.

From the small beginnings at Wharncliffe War Hospital, to the times when production methods became more sophisticated:-

Production required a variation of light work, and it was possible for the men to carry out tasks through painting, cutting out, packing and finishing. Men could take up a wide variety of positions and work.

"People do not buy our goods from charity but because they like beautiful things," she would claim. "The men mix their own colours from basic dyes and the colour schemes and designs are the work of artists which have been provided voluntarily. The work is sold at exhibitions and by post. The men are paid for their work and pay a small rent for their houses, where they live with their families."

Work as mental therapy

The basic idea of productive rehabilitation was supported by a number of influential organisations. The Council of Trustees of the Douglas Haig Memorial Homes were providing groups of dwellings in several large centres of population, rather than in country districts, because it is important that their beneficiaries, ex-servicemen and their widows shall have the opportunity of employment for themselves and their families.

She usually let the 'impossible' tasks performed and skills displayed speak for themselves through the quality and range of products produced and sold.

Balancing the books

She never hid the reality that survival was always a problem. Growth was a necessity given the increasing numbers of men who wanted to come to Painted Fabrics once the word got around.

Finances were always tight, and sales and what we describe today as marketing prospects had to be energetically and creatively pursued.

Despite all its idealism, the hard financial realities of an independent business had to be faced. There was a regular financial crisis at the end of the week when wages had to be paid. Undoubtedly there were times when Annie's husband bailed them out. The company was subsidised for years later on in its life, but they carried on.

She confronted all and sundry that she came across and those with whom she could engineer a meeting with the grim realities of her charges, in order that their purse strings might be loosened or their hearts could be touched, but never in a sentimental or patronising way and always with a specific and practical purpose in mind. She set out to appeal to their better judgement and perhaps make them feel a little guilty in their privileged position, detached somewhat from the atrocities of the War.

Yet always her business plan and strategy was focused and targeted, as well designed and executed as any current business school model.

She may have been addressed by some as 'Binnie' and signed off her letters 'A.B.C.' after Annie Bindon Carter in an endearing way with a completely unstuffy manner and with a total lack of pomposity, but her business dealings were cool, detached and quite calculating.

She was nothing if not ambitious, as illustrated in one letter sent to Lieutenant Colonel Crosfield on the 5th of November 1928. When better than Bonfire night to light a few fires?

'I enclose to you a further series of rough notes putting forth my claim to the possibility of finding employment for at least 100 more ex-servicemen. It would, of course, entail an enormous lot of hard work and organisation but we are perfectly prepared for this. As stated in my previous letter I am most anxious for as many members of the British Legion Committee as possible to come up to 'Painted Fabrics' in order to see exactly what we are doing and where we are doing it'.

Counting the cost

In applying for funding in 1927 she wrote:

"It would be our intention to use any monies placed in our charge to provide work and make a profit which would be kept in the business, enabling us to establish a permanent trade. To this end we would need to increase stock, and buy materials in bulk in order to obtain advantageous prices. Our recent turnover in 1927 of £19,701 was looked after by a very small number of office staff of three men and one filing clerk. This could have been very much better attended to with double that number but lack of capital prevented more being employed.

The question of increased turnover also increases the number of men required in the Making-Up Departments. At the present time we have two men working on machines hemming, stitching up, picot edging and so forth. We could employ more but at present have to put work out in the way of cushion covers etc. to be made up because of this lack of available capital for purchasing machines [electric hem stitching machines costing approximately £76 each]. Exactly the same procedure could be worked out for the lampshade trade, an article which we are asked for frequently, and which we have done very successfully when we have had a special order from a customer. We have facilities for decorating with our stencilling and spray painting which no other firm has. Then there is the question of screens. From time to time we have received orders for these screens which we have carried out and for which we have received much praise. We were asked for screens as early as 1919 from home manufacturers but of course we have never been able to show them. We endeavoured to put on the market screen panels but to be worth anything they must be made up and designed – panelled and framed in one, in order to make up a perfect article. This work would require two or three carpenters, capable of doing simple woodwork

and making up original ideas which could be worked out for them.
All these trades are not new to us but are being carried out at the present time in a 'slipshod'
manner, unavoidable on account of the lack of capital."

The making of a businesswoman

She was a quietly spoken, gentle, modest and charming force of nature. Small in stature but with a heart as big as a bucket, as they would say in her adopted Sheffield – although she moved in the swankiest of circles in order to promote her beloved Painted Fabrics.

She was an entrepreneur, the creator of an initiative, a pioneer, an innovator and designer, a visionary and practitioner and above all a warm-hearted woman in a tiny frame, determined and dedicated to help men whose fate had charted that their paths should cross and who benefitted greatly from this serendipity.

She fought hard for her 'men' on every front, even arguing on their behalf with the Income Tax authorities. She wrote "Profits are used in every case to find employment for further men. From the commencement of Painted Fabrics to the present time, there has been a long waiting list of disabled men anxious to come to the workshop".

Pioneers are often characterised by their reluctance to let go or to admit their initiative's time had come. The inevitability of closure was finally recognised in 1957. Despite all the socialising, Annie Bindon Carter never lost sight of Painted Fabrics' prime motive: to provide meaningful work and jobs.

She strongly admonished her audience (including those that did not turn up) after bleak weather had hit the turnout of the 1937 Christmas show at the Queens Hotel in Leeds.

"If these men had not gone to fight for us during the war it is doubtful whether we would all be sitting here today in the warmth and comfort of this hotel," she told them sternly, "It is no excuse for people to say they cannot come because of the weather. These men had to go over the top in all kinds of weather."

Who's looking after the shop?

The legal requirements of a Limited Company required a properly constituted structure and Painted Fabrics quickly established its own.

At the top Painted Fabrics had Board of Directors (with directors, chairman, secretary and treasurer), a Committee and a designated group of official Patrons. Formal and thoroughly business-like relationships were established with the bank, government departments, local authorities, charities and funding bodies.

Painted Fabrics quickly developed into a much more differentiated organisation with formal relationships, an established structure to carry out work tasks, which in turn were becoming more interlinked and complex, and most important to meet legal requirements and operate successfully in the business world, a new business, limited company structure.

The organisational structure became layered and functional, each tier having certain prescribed and defined purposes and functions. Along with this came a whole plethora of new positions and titles, including works manager and foreman. Separate departments were set up in the Production area including the Main Workshop, the SASMA Room and the Leather Department.

Different departments were set up for different products and processes, each with their own management and supervisory staff, foremen and assistants. Business titles were used and responsibilities allocated, suitable people were recruited and appointed, and wage and salary systems established and maintained.

Business in style

Sales brochures were prepared, shops opened and staffed, exhibitions held, sales drives embarked upon and many other trappings of a thoroughly modern business were added.

The men who joined were picked out for particular jobs and roles according to their background and suitability, skills and capacities. It was a case of from each according to their ability, and everyone, yes everyone, was capable of making a contribution. Officers and Non Commissioned Officers were not to be left out.

"During the years 1923-25 a great deal of the selling was done by me," wrote Annie Bindon Carter, *"with the direct idea of making positions for salesmen. This objective has gradually been achieved. Three ex-Officers and two Sergeant Majors now being employed on this work"*.

Organisational structures were hierarchical to match those in the rest of society, business or otherwise. All this organisation structure, functionality, responsibility and formality was in direct contrast to the more informal, personal contact basis of the other side of Painted Fabrics, that is its volunteer basis and the support and endorsement through personal contacts friendships and relationships with the gentry, nobility and even royalty of the day. With one it was 'what you know', with the other definitely 'who you know.'

Painted Fabrics took on its new Corporate Identity in 1924, and Annie Bindon Carter's ambition was fulfilled. They were now a proper business, in a proper industry, and people would take them seriously.

She quickly established a complete range of arrangements, formal positions and bureaucratic procedures which any business entity would have been proud of no matter what position and trade they were in, what size they were or experience they had.

They would look like a business and act like one, albeit a rather special one. From the beginning the company was to be firmly wedded to a clear understanding of the basis of the business it was involved in, the fullest expression possible of the highest principles of Art and Design, meticulously applied to the production of high fashion goods of the best quality. From the very beginning of Cpl. Wallwork's cushion cover stencils, over this there was to be no compromise – it was to be high quality, stunning design and artistic in essence. There was a fundamental belief that although the men of Painted Fabrics may have been severely damaged in body (and in some cases mind), their ego and finer sensitivities could still be cultivated and put to use for the finest of artistic and pleasing purposes. The whole ambition of it all required an enormous act of faith and a belief in the indomitable spirit of the people they were dealing with. Time and time again they were proved gloriously right.

The business from top to bottom

The new Painted Fabrics letterhead proudly announced that several notable dignitaries would be behind the new enterprise:

Patronage
H.M. Queen Elizabeth, the Queen Mother
Patron
Her Royal Highness, the Princess Royal
Vice Patrons
Her Grace, the Duchess of Beaufort,
Maud, Countess Fitzwilliam
The Marchioness of Bute,
The Dowager Countess Jellicoe

Directing the business
Business Leaders, Captains of Industry and local dignitaries were recruited as directors, such as:-
Sir Ashley S. Ward, LL. D,

W. W. Wood, Esq., JP II.,

J. Staines, Esq., J.P.,

R L. Walsh, Esq., F.C.A.,

Peter Macgregor,

Mr. J. H. Doncaster,

Captain Donald Simpson,

Hon. Sec. Mr Geoffrey C. Carter,

Captain L. P. Scott [Sales Manager].

How are we managing?

Running the company on the Management Committee were:-

All the directors and:-

Sir John Rosenstein, CBE., PhD,

W.D. Brooks, Esq.,

Mr Peter Macgregor [Chairman],

The Right Reverend, the Lord Bishop of Sheffield,

Colonel Sir Charles Clifford K.B.E., Mr Geoffrey Carter,

The Countess Fitzwilliam,

Mr W.W. Chisholm J.P.,

Mrs Leonard Burrows M.B.E.,

Captain Donald Simpson,

Mr H.I. Potter,

Mrs. A.B. Carter [Hon. Secretary] [later O.B.E.],

Irene Clegg was Painted Fabrics' Secretary in the 1930s.

and to add a final element of necessary gravitas…

BANKERS WILLIAMS DEACONS Bank LTD.

It was emphasised that *"all administrative staff and the council which runs Painted Fabrics do not draw a penny in either wages or expenses and all profits are ploughed back into the company for further development"*.

A learning company

Painted Fabrics was an organisation of extreme contrasts. On the one hand a workable, logical, symbiosis of styles and ways of working, on the other a one-off anachronistic jumble of ideas and management practices. And what was an opportunist amateur doing cobbling together such an organisation? No background, no qualifications (although few examinations had to be passed to embark on a career in business in those days, it has to be said). Not even attendance at the right school or family connections. Nevertheless she helped develop a viable, visionary business model in the most difficult of times – the achievement of a true pioneer. But handsome is what handsome does in the real world, and fabrics and for the most part Painted Fabrics worked well as a business.

Training especially was something that Painted Fabrics felt it had to pay close attention to and eventually excelled in, often helping people to learn to do things they would not have deemed possible under any other circumstances. Limbless men learned subtle and artistic physical skills such as stencilling, cutting out and printing, as shown in the following letter:-

78 Lansdowne Road, Bournemouth
7th February 1917

Dear Mrs Carter,
Your letter regarding Robert Grindel, to be trained.
I think we could train the man for you but it is difficult to say how long it would take, as though you say simple screens it might mean joinery, which means careful fitting. It would also entail a certain amount of waste in material while teaching the man. I don't suppose it would be much but we could not afford the money, but I dare say Painted Fabrics would repay this.
Then, as regards pay for him whilst under training. This also we could not afford as we would not be keeping the man for future work with us. We usually pay such cases 6d an hour. The greatest difficulty, and one I don't know how to overcome, is where the man is to live whilst undergoing training. It is most difficult and very expensive to find accommodation here, as though there are many who let rooms the prices are very high and they can easily get what they are asking from mid-March to mid-October, as so many come here from the Midlands for their

holidays. Perhaps this man, as he is an Isle of Wight man, has friends and can arrange this difficult problem himself. If we do train him we would like a sample frame on loan to show us what is required, to see what sort of joinery is required and the amount of smoothing and planning that would be necessary.

H. T. Brooking

Men similarly disabled carrying out demanding and responsible supervisory and management roles and functions.

The most incapable

In 1949 Mrs Carter sent a letter to the Board of Trade appealing against the imposition of Purchase Tax and claiming exemption for Painted Fabrics on the grounds of 'unusual circumstances applying to the company.' In designing, producing and selling Painted Fabrics goods, huge disadvantages had to be overcome compared with more conventional businesses and this case was argued in a long letter which shows graphically the ABC mixture of deep sensitivity and humanity and a sharp business-like approach which does not miss a trick in pleading her men's and the company's case:

12th January 1949
Purchase tax exemption. The choice of the luxury craft [on which the Painted Fabrics business is based] was first made because we were able to employ men in this work who had lost both hands. Later it was found to be particularly suitable for double amputations [legs], loss of one arm and one leg, loss of two legs and an arm, disseminating sclerosis and other nerve troubles. The dyeing, washing and fastening of colour is done by men who have lost one leg, but require added care owing to having in the past suffered from such illnesses as TB and heart trouble in addition to the amputations. The whole purpose of Painted Fabrics is to enable these men to live once more, to have the power to earn money and to feel independent. The following are some of Painted Fabrics' problems:-

1. A man of the First World War, minus both legs and having become very heavy, suffered severe heart troubles and was ill for many months. His doctor suggested he should return to the workshop for one to two hours per day. We put him onto patterning small handkerchiefs, and six of these were put into a box and sold for 19/ 6d a box. The man took 2 to 3 hours to produce one handkerchief – practically the whole of the money was wages and yet we must pay purchase tax.

2. A torpedoed sailor, left in an open boat for 10 days and cast upon the Brazilian coast – this man, owing to nerve shock of a most distressing kind, works only occasionally and very erratically. How is it possible to pay purchase tax on the finishing of small mats which should take a few minutes but sometimes might take hours?

3. Or the other extreme – Two young boys from the recent war, both having lost both legs, are so thankful to find something to do, that they are in a constant state of desiring to beat all records, but not always producing the highest standard of workmanship. In patterning long lengths of furnishing materials which are 48ins wide, we have, in the past, come up against the following problem:

The two young men with no legs are able to sit on the table to work and so reach the centre of the 48ins material. Two men of WWI – one of them a double amputation of legs, the other with the loss of one leg, the other at right angles completely stiff – could work along the sides of the table but were not able to stretch.

However another medical difficulty arose. These young men must wear their artificial limbs as much as possible, but when they do the possibility of reaching the centre of the table again arises. Therefore, from time to time we cut the material in half and produce cushion covers, thus overcoming the stretching problem.

However the material printed all over at that time carries no purchase tax, but when made into cushion covers carries tax. Our purpose is only to employ the "unemployable" and in the past, when taking on a new man, we have always chosen the man with the worst disability and not, as an ordinary firm would do, the most capable."

The developing organisation

Using this basic structure Painted Fabrics traded successfully for forty years from 1917 to 1957, experiencing difficult post-war conditions, through the greatest economic depression the world had ever known with mass unemployment and recession, followed by yet another brutal World War, and a difficult post-war recovery. The task of creating and maintaining jobs for disabled men was challenging at a time when countless thousands of able-bodied men had no work at all, and appropriately developing the business as they went along to meet demanding changing circumstances.

What is more there were no business models for Painted Fabrics to copy. Yet Annie Bindon Carter was more than able to steer the ship through troubled waters by having a rock-solid basis of principles to follow and a canny knack of getting her way. Many, many businesses failed during this long and difficult period whilst Painted Fabrics managed to carry on without any state subsidy or aid, a major economic miracle in itself, despite the 1930s and the Great Depression where working men, able-bodied or not, were struggling to find jobs.

Painted Fabrics was suspended during WWII and its workshops turned over to making aircraft parts.

The art of Painted Fabrics

In Their Finery

"Working under skilled fashion artists and designers, the men decorate materials which are then made up into gowns, shawls, rest gowns, dress lengths, scarves, lingerie, happy coats, bridge coats and cloaks, curtains, table cloths, cushion covers, bedspreads, fancy bags etc.

In addition a section of the factory is devoted to dye material, block printing and manufacturing leather work."

Painted Fabrics had become a fashion house of some reputation from its small beginnings in a grim post-war industrial northern city through its noble patronage and connections, its innovative designs and quality craftsmanship and efficient leadership and management. Behind the rather jolly and somewhat 'amateurish'

approach to design and art on the surface there lay a much more serious professional intent and practice in the work of Painted Fabrics, as the young artists from Sheffield College were joined by others who found a fertile ground for their talents.

Sheffield had already established a formidable reputation and background in the 'Arts and Crafts' movement, largely through the presence in the city for ten years of one of the founders and main characters, John Ruskin, who started and ran the St. George's Centre at Crookes, set high on the hills above the heavy industry of Sheffield at that time.

Edward Carpenter, writer and campaigner for homosexual rights, who also had strong connections with the trade unions and broader labour movement, lived and worked in Sheffield and was visited by many writers and artists including Annie Besant, Madame Blavatsky and Olive Shreiner, all of whom alongside many others contributed to create the melting pot of artistic and design influences on Painted Fabrics.

This eventually produced the distinctive and original collection of designs which were unmistakably Painted Fabrics in origin and production.

The men who actually produced the Painted Fabrics materials and products, given their background, recent traumatic experiences and unique set of skills and capacities (not to say their methods of working), must have added their own creativity and personality to the work.

A peasant industry

In 1938, Dr Rothernstein was appointed Director of the Tate Gallery in London. He was former Director of Sheffield Art Galleries and member of the Advisory Committee of Painted Fabrics. His connection and commitment to Painted Fabrics was well known and helped to further Sheffield's cause in London art and couture circles.

Painted Fabrics was described as a:

"new and interesting English peasant industry. The designs are the work of artists which have been contributed voluntarily. Their goods of high quality, in original designs and colour schemes, have already made their reputation."

Annie Bindon Carter gave a speech on 'Peasant Industry' which explained in some detail the origins of the unique Painted Fabrics approach.

"The designs suggested by me are adapted from many sources and are of necessity grown by force of circumstances, mainly due to disability and partly due to what I will call 'Peasant Outlook'.

Dr. Rohenstein, the Director of the Tate Gallery, always stresses this point in any remarks he has made publicly related to Painted Fabrics. His point in every case has been that Painted Fabrics was developing a new and English peasant industry and that the patterning so evolved was of intense historical interest – as in all matters relating to art, the suggestion of whether you like the work or not is debatable and personal. I may say here that Dr. Rohenstein is the only person who has completely understood Painted Fabrics' work. To compare the design of articles produced by these ex-servicemen with shall we say Courtaulds' marvellous and accurate productions, or those stocked in Harrods, is a complete lack of understanding of the problem.

I am convinced we require no more machinery – we are very well equipped for our purpose. The men are clever and industrious and intensely interested in their work.

Of great assistance would be an Austrian refugee used to working amongst the Austrian peasant textile industries – a designer and also of sufficient technical knowledge.

Any of the modern slick machine patterns are impossible for us to produce. To compare Painted Fabrics with any of these is like comparing Old English pewter work with modern electro-plated goods. Some old pewter work was artistically worthless, some artistic treasures are all of interest. I am quite sure Lord Fitzwilliam has not hung Painted Fabrics curtains beside De Laszlo pictures and priceless artefacts in his main living room for the last fourteen years for charity's sake, nor did Mrs Bebag Montefiore equip her new house with Painted Fabrics curtains at the cost of several hundred pounds for this reason – but because of their artistic value."

Designed in Sheffield

The design of the patterns used in the fabric and clothes range at Painted Fabrics was first undertaken by Annie Bindon Carter who had shown exhibition of paintings at the London Portrait Society. She was assisted by her sister Dorothy and by Edith Jagger (sister of Charles Sergeant Jagger the sculptor and David Jagger the painter). All three women studied at the Sheffield School of Art.

Edith Jagger had been amongst those who helped at the Wharncliffe War Hospital, where she worked as a volunteer, particularly to help the men who were subject to fits as a result of head wounds, working with them locked in a padded room. No doubt she was untrained in this kind of work, as precious few were, as they tried to cope with the flood of survivors from the war, badly wounded physically and in turmoil mentally. She would be unqualified to undertake this kind of work and certainly not officially appointed by any authority, but carried out her work doing the best she could out of her own training and family background, her common humanity and a desire to help the poor broken men as best she could, as did all the others.

She was born in Kilnhurst, near Rotherham, the daughter of a colliery manager. She attended Sheffield School of Art and was an accomplished artist in her own right specialising in landscapes and still life, especially flowers which can be seen in Painted Fabrics' original designs.

After 1918 she was more officially employed as a designer at Painted Fabrics, now contributing with the advantage of hands on experience of the kind of challenges men would face and practical ideas on how to overcome these in the production of new products to meet the demands of a growing list of customers.

Edith had two brothers who also attended the Sheffield School of Art and became internationally-noted artists.

David Jagger became a leading member of the Royal Institute of Oil painters, and exhibited regularly at both the Royal Academy and the Royal Society of British Artists. His obituary, after he died in 1958, described him as:-

"a fashionable society painter who combined the ability to catch a likeness with meticulous craftsmanship."

But it was Edith's eldest brother, Charles Sargeant Jagger, who provided the most graphic family reflection of Edith's work with the disabled soldiers of World War I at Painted Fabrics. Charles Sargeant Jagger MC was born on the 17th of December 1885 in Kilnhurst. At the tender age of 14 he became an apprentice metal engraver with the Sheffield firm Mappin and Webb. He studied at the Sheffield School of Art before moving to London to study sculpture at the Royal College of Art from 1908 to 1911. His student work won him a travelling scholarship which took him to Rome and Venice. In 1914 he won the British Prix de Rome. When war broke out in 1914, Charles Sargeant Jagger gave up his Rome scholarship to join the Army. At first he joined the Artist's Rifles, and in 1915 he was commissioned in the Worcestershire Regiment. He served in Gallipoli and on the Western Front and was wounded three times. He was awarded the Military Cross for gallantry. It was during one of his convalescent periods that he first helped the Painted Fabrics design team. Jagger's sculpturing style tended towards realism, especially his portrayal of soldiers. His figures were rugged and workmanlike, earning him a reputation for 'realist' sculpture. It was for his dramatic and moving war memorials that he was chiefly remembered.

Whilst convalescing from war wounds in 1919, he began work on 'No Man's Land', a low relief which is today part of the Tate collection. It depicts a 'listening post', a technique of trench warfare in which a soldier would hide amongst the corpses, broken stretchers and barbed wire, in order to listen for the enemy.

His best-known studies are with us today, in the most prominent and popular places, confronting those who see with the reality of the challenge that his sister and many others had to face as a consequence of war. The Royal Artillery Memorial at Hyde Park Corner features a giant sculpture of a howitzer surrounded by four bronze soldiers. When making the piece he commented:-

"My experience of the trenches persuaded me of the necessity of frankness and truth."

During the war years government edict had forbidden images of dead British soldiers being shown. Jagger defied these instructions by creating realistic figures of standing soldiers and the body of a dead soldier laid out and shrouded by a greatcoat. Other works included a statue of a soldier reading a letter from home, two stone statues of machine gunners, a soldier wearing a greatcoat and helmet, holding a bayonet, a hooded woman and an infantry soldier holding a bayonet rifle, soldiers fighting and carrying the wounded in the trenches, a driver holding a horse bridle and a British Infantry soldier standing guard with rifle and bayonet.

Charles Sargeant Jagger died suddenly of pneumonia in 1934.

The Painted Fabrics way

The characteristic artistic and design style which emerged at Painted Fabrics began with Annie Bindon Carter, Edith Jagger and other staff and students of Sheffield Art College who assisted at the Wharncliffe War Hospital in the formative days. An eclectic approach followed which at first sight did not seem to owe much to Edith Jagger's brothers or other First World War artists such as Nash.

The origins of the 'Painted Fabrics' design style seemed at first to owe more to Sheffield Art College and other more student and academic origins than the graphic realism of 'war' artists and designers.

Ostensibly it might also seem unlikely that men of Painted Fabrics, using their newly acquired skills in transforming designs into useable products, could have contributed much to their artistic quality out of their background and recent wartime

experiences, but not impossible as we look at the fabulous products of serving soldiers, created as so-called 'Trench' Art, by Allied and German forces.

What is clear is that no one style or pattern predominated. Customers were offered a product which was the result of many different, complex and distinctive influences feeding into the design and production of Painted Fabrics wares, as the first germ of an idea began to be formulated through to the final display at the shop or show in front of potential customers.

The fashionable designs first produced of stylised botanical subjects were chiefly the work of Edith Jagger and Annie Bindon Carter working with Mr. Goodrich.

In those early days financial help was sought to equip the work room with dye vats, steamers, block printing tables, materials etc. Ironically before Printed Fabrics entered the market most of this kind of merchandise came from Germany.

Stencilling and block printing were fashionable means of decoration and formed the basis of their studies. With the incentive of a packet of Woodbines, neat and accurate work was produced by the men. Single repeat stencil patterns were painted onto cleaned and stretched canvas sacks to produce 'Zepp curtains'.

Watercolour designs, Old English scenes and Indian patterns, along with scenes from history and mythology, secular and saintly, and play scenes from "Mr. Shakespeare", were all used.

The artistic and design style of Painted Fabrics derived its inspiration from many and varied sources. The results were distinctive designs and natural patterns depicting traditional scenes; aspects of a rural and country idyll; botanical themes; classical scenes and images; religious, patriotic and regal subjects; Modernist and Impressionist influences; and even abstract, stylised approaches and motifs were used.

"Ladies in Stencilled Dresses"

From the SHEFFIELD TELEGRAPH:

"Exquisite soft shades were stencilled on the material which was made up with a grey border and a tiny front panel of white, upon which was a row of buttons of the palest amethyst.

The type of merchandise produced by Painted Fabrics shows a practical and modern use of an ancient fine arts process for the decoration, not only of hangings, wall coverings, and 'cloths of state', to use an Elizabethan phrase, but of various articles of household use, adornment and personal wear.

The designs, entirely original, are from the hands of English artists of the foremost standing in the field of decorative design.

Their colour schemes, often strikingly original, are yet entirely harmonious, whilst the craftsmanship involved in their execution is pronounced by leading authorities who have examined their work to be of the highest order."

"Ladies in Stencilled Dresses." attracted many potential buyers to Painted Fabrics.

Buyers were immediately reminded that before Painted Fabrics entered the market "This kind of merchandise previously came from the hands of our late enemies." To emphasise the patriotic point potential buyers were reminded that:-

"In buying the merchandise of Painted Fabrics you are:-

1. Buying British, and

2. Helping the men who gave their health and strength to keep the Empire British, and enabling them to enjoy that independence for which they fought."

At no time did Annie Bindon Carter and her team lose sight of what Painted Fabrics had been set up to do, what it meant for all those who lived and worked there and the countless many who leant there encouragement and support. To achieve these laudable aims they had to be serious in intent and practice, particularly in the areas of production and design.

Tasteful and attractive designs were essential, but Painted Fabrics were more ambitious than that – they also wanted to be stylish and innovative.

Painted Fabrics designs were an apparently haphazard mix of Bohemian sophistication, Eastern European peasant art, Jazz age gaiety and Pageantry, with the odd chintzy hint of Merrie England, using the sort of flimsy textures favoured by Matisse and fellow Fauvist artists which somehow produced a coherent Painted Fabrics style.

An eclectic mixture

The subject matter, images, colours and patterns used by William Morris, Ruskin and the Arts and Craft movement around at the time can be clearly seen, but many others were also introduced. Nothing can be said to dominate, but it made for an exciting, innovative and easily recognisable approach which won Painted Fabrics many friends and followers.

The products were often strikingly beautiful, with unexpected colour combinations and emblematic designs, favouring lilies, hollyhocks, sleek angels, pseudo-heraldry, pensive knights and even abstract dogs.

It was proudly and extensively advertised that 'the colour schemes and designs are the work of artists which have been provided voluntarily, in colours and patterns which delight the eye'.

Painted Fabrics by design

From the very beginning the products of Painted Fabrics were very strongly influenced by concepts and aspirations of innovative and high class designs. It could hardly have been otherwise given the interests and professional standards of Annie Bindon Carter and her art school friends. The degree to which they were able to establish and maintain – even exceed – their initial plans, given the limitations and lack of any experience of the men who arrived at Wharncliffe Hospital, was admirable and astonishing. Starting with ABC herself, her colleagues described her as *"an artist of a kind way ahead of her time. She was doing stuff in the 1920s which was to become all the vogue in the 1960s and early 70s. She was into these designs, outlandish some of them. But she gathered round her friends who were of the same artistic temperament."*

One of them was Edith Jagger:

"From the beginning the style of Painted Fabrics designs was very varied, but the bold and brilliant colour combinations and the fluid use of fabric in their designs for clothing were very much in tune with the period, showing the influence of Fauves painters such as Matisse and Dufy and the excitement of the Oriental, inspired by Diaghilev's Ballets Russes."

Curtains of Oriental design were particularly requested by Messrs. Goodall of

www.picturesheffield.com

Manchester who were exhibiting Painted Fabrics goods in their shop windows as early as July 1918.

A more bohemian influence reflecting the peasant costumes of Eastern Europe can be seen in much of the bright floral decoration on shawls which could be worn in the gypsy style over full skirts and on scarves which might be wrapped around the head.

Although hand stencilling using paints formed the mainstay of production, screen printing, block printing and spray painting with dyes was also used.

The fabrics, which ranged from 'crash' (coarse linen) to silk, satin, chiffon and velvet for the luxury end of the market, were originally brought in a finished state, but within a few years were bought raw and bleached and dyed in the workshops. As the quality of rayon (or artificial silk as it was called) improved, this was added to the range of fabrics, widening the design possibilities and being used for some of the more profitable dress goods. Much of the making up was done on the premises. The men did most of the stitching using specially adapted sewing machines, although some of their wives and daughters were also employed as seamstresses under the direction of professional dressmakers who did the cutting out.

There was a conventional sophistication in some of PF's other patterns and clothes such as men's silk handkerchiefs and dressing gowns for the luxury end of the market. Day dresses, which included bridal wear, were especially commissioned, as were alter frontals and other fabrics for churches, work for theatrical productions and a variety of furnishings for private houses.

Aspects of William Morris's design style can be seen in Painted Fabric compositions and themes. There was similarly a considerable overlap in the range of products for which designs were used.

Morris's 'River' chintz textile designs from the 1880s such as the Cray and the Wandle are strongly reflected in Painted Fabric textile designs, as were later designs such as the Rose and Thistle, the Tulip and the Willow, and the Bluebell/Columbine.

His designs for tapestries included Woodpecker, the Annunciation and the Forest, wall hangings, including the Acanthus, the Lotus and the Artichoke, and curtains, such as the Honeysuckle, the Peacock and the Dragon and his 'Bird' curtains. Morris's most appreciated themes, stories and images such as the Tree Heroines, Guinevere, the Knights of the Round Table, the Minstrel and Woman Playing a Lute and the Orchard (the Seasons) are redolent of Painted Fabrics, as were religious themes such as the Vision of the Holy Grail and the adoration of the Magi.

Markets for Printed Fabrics products included Spain, Italy, Belgium, Greece, India, Canada, the West Indies and New York.

Some 20 years ago, archivist Ruth Harman opened a hitherto forgotten cardboard box abandoned in a storeroom labelled 'Painted Fabrics', which contained gold curtains, lovely dresses in their original boxes and handkerchiefs, all glowing with vibrant colours.

Fabrics for Painting

Fabrics used were also suitably glamorous, sophisticated and stylish as appropriate for the selective market Painted Fabrics had targeted.

They included French crêpe, a fabric of silk or wool with a distinctly crisp, crumpled appearance; and chiffon, from the French word for cloth or rag – a balanced, plain, woven sheer fabric, made from alternate crêpe yarns. The twist in the crêpe yarns puckers the fabric after weaving, giving it some stretch and a slightly rough feel, and some enticing see-through properties.

Suiting the Painted Fabrics requirements, chiffon could be dyed to almost any shade. Chiffon was mostly used in evening wear, especially as an overlay, giving an elegant and floating appearance to the gown. Chiffon was also used in the production of blouses, scarves and lingerie. We have a picture of a 1922 morning dress in chiffon and lace.

Silks in many forms including charmeuse, taffeta, crêpe de chine and shantung for bridal gowns, were used prolifically by Painted Fabrics designers, primarily for clothing, especially ties, blouses and pyjamas, but also made up into robes, sundresses and costumes. The attractive lustre and drape of silk made it a fabric most suitable for furnishings, wall hangings rugs and bedding.

Satins, with their glossy surface and dull backs, were also very popular with Painted Fabrics' customers, used extensively for bed sheets, women's lingerie nightgowns, evening gowns, blouses and men's neck ties, and also for some interior furnishings and upholstery.

Damask was another Painted Fabric material – the reversible, figured fabric of silk, wool, linen or cotton emanating originally from the Byzantine and Islamic weaving centres of the 14th Century in Europe.

Linen and flax were other sought-after materials used in many forms by the craftsmen of the company. Cool and fresh, linen was fashioned into bedlinen, tablecloths, runners and chair covers through to shirts, chemises and even waistcoats. Calico was a plain woven textile made from unbleached cotton. Coarse and thick, the raw fabric was dyed and printed in attractive, bright hues.

Brocade was another of Painted Fabrics' favourite cloths to work with, creating coloured and embossed silks resembling tapestry and used in upholstery and draperies. Brocades were also especially adapted for evening and formal clothing and special costumes.

Clothes produced included chiffon and crêpe de chine dresses.

This wide range of fabric products, as well as being made up on the premises, were often sold as lengths to be made up later by others.

Pink slips, green belts, shawls, and even a priest's stole were also made.

Nothing to wear madame?

The designers at Painted Fabrics were not slow to advise and educate their customers as publicity brochures indicated:-

"The type of merchandise produced by "Painted Fabrics" shows a practical and a modern use of an ancient fine arts process for the decoration, not only of hangings, wall coverings and 'Elizabethan' cloths of state, but of various articles of household use, adornment and household ware. The designs, entirely original, are from the hands of English artists of the foremost standing in the field of decorative design."

Their colour schemes, often strikingly original, are yet harmonious, while the craftsmanship involved in their execution is pronounced by leading authorities who have examined the work to be of the highest order.

Working under skilled fashion artists and designers, the men decorate materials which are then made up into gowns, shawls, rest gowns, dress lengths, scarves, lingerie, happy coats, bridge coats, cloaks, curtains, tablecloths, cushion covers, bedspreads, fancy bags etc.

In addition a section of the factory is devoted to dyeing material, block printing and manufacturing leather work."

Dress goods were made from painted and block printed silk crêpe de chine and georgette, and gold and silver tissue cloth.

Personal clothing items such as handkerchiefs and scarves, decorated capes and shawls, pyjamas, rest gowns and night gowns were produced and sold well.

Other items included Mappie Coats, happy coats, bridge coats, cloaks, kimonos, dress lengths and lingerie.

Home decorations?

Ideas and suggestions for decorations and soft furnishings using Painted Fabrics materials and designs offered by their designers were many and varied. They included:-

"Fine materials and fabrics made up into curtains, lunettes and banners, wall hangings for [stately] homes and castles, theatre stage hangings and whole sets,"
"Church interiors and alter cloths, and panels",

"Tapestries and table cloths, furnishings and furniture coverings, chair backs, runners and cushion covers,"
"Bedspreads and tablecloths,"

Later novelty items, luncheon sets, dressing table sets, table mats, ties and bedspreads, tea cosies luncheon sets, dressing table sets, tea cosies fur trimmed coats and fancy bags and other leather goods were added to the range when the work room was short of orders.

Everything was designed and made up on site, "Made in Sheffield" with as much satisfaction and pride as any of the finest stainless steel or cutlery.

Items were dyed and stencilled, painted, screen printed and block printed. Undyed materials were used also.

Selling painted fabrics

The main way of selling was through exhibitions, of which there were two types:- Firstly, those held in town or public halls where some of the men would help the volunteers to sell. Although these were labour intensive and quite expensive to organise, they were felt to be an effective way of reaching large numbers of ordinary people and selling less expensive items such as scarves and cushion covers. The first exhibition was held at Wharncliffe Hospital and the last one in the Cutler's Hall. In the intervening years hundreds were held up and down the country as well as abroad. The second type of exhibition was the "At Homes", held by the aristocratic ladies Annie Bindon Carter had so successfully recruited as supporters of Painted Fabrics. Some of these were held in their own houses (Wentworth Woodhouse every year); others were held in suites in large hotels. As a Sheffield newspaper reported in 1937, "The Exhibition at Claridges is firmly established as one of the principal events of the season and it deserves to be, for neither Bond Street nor the Rue de Paix can show articles which excel either in quality or perfection of workmanship of these Painted Fabrics products."

The SASMATIAN of July 1932 reported on the success of the season's programme:-

"June 1932 has been a month of triumph for 'Sasmatian Craftsmen'. Our annual Summer Exhibition at Claridges beat all previous records and though there was not a square foot of empty space during the 3 hours of the "private view" we were in the extraordinary position of having to turn away more people than we admitted. By the end of May we already had as many acceptances to fill the ballroom suite at Claridges, and we had to circularise the social editors of the national daily newspapers, not to mention the "Private View" in their news columns. We are told by the social editor of a great national newspaper that this is the first time in his twenty years' experience that he has ever heard of such a request being made. Our fame can only spread through the goodwill of our past customers, and therefore we consider the increasing success of our Annual Summer Exhibition to be due to the enthusiastic way in which you have been talking about us to your friends and we offer to you our sincere thanks."

A long, long way indeed from the steelworks back streets of Sheffield, the trenches of the Somme and the workshops and new homes at Meadowhead.

The SASMATIAN, now in full pomp, trumpets on:-

"Our next big Exhibition is the War Disabled Men's Exhibition at the Imperial Institute from November 8th to 25th and we are already working for a greater success than ever, but we are just as anxious to run big and successful exhibitions in August, September and October and we earnestly appeal to you to help us with suggestions. Our June and November exhibitions keep the men busy for a month or six weeks beforehand, but we want to keep them busy throughout the year by running a super exhibition every month. If we had plenty of capital and could employ a large staff of salespeople. We do not anticipate there would be any difficulty in organising a successful super-exhibition every month, but we have very little available capital, which forces us to rely on voluntary effort, and this is where you can be such a tremendous force and help if only you would realise it.

One of our customers living in a tiny village in Oxfordshire sends us more than 200 pounds worth of business per annum because she never misses an opportunity of mentioning our work to her friends wherever she may be. If only 99 other people would enlist our services in the same way this would keep our men in steady work throughout the year."

"Old readers will observe that we republish extracts so that new readers are told something about the early days of the industry and its development."

"THE WAY OF THE WORLD - NO FAIRY GODMOTHER"

"Think of the return you would get in satisfaction buying our merchandise, to think that by your action ex-private Tommy Atkins, minus both legs and a right arm, was able to hobble to his little home on a Friday night with his well-earned wage packet, and with a smile on his face tell his wife that she could have that new coat, as owing to the large number of orders received, he would be busy again next week."

Phyllis Lawton remembers the very grandest sales, however, were staged in London at the Claridges Hotel.

"Mrs Carter used all the contacts she could to make sure they were well-attended and a success. The Queen regularly attended the sales. It was what one did during the summer season in those days: Ascot, Henley, Wimbledon and Painted Fabrics sales. You particularly wanted to be seen there if you had a title. The guest list for the sale of 1932 included:-

The Marchioness Linlithgow, the Viscountess Plummer, the Duchess of Buccleuch, Priscilla Countess Annesley, Lady Harriet Bunbury, Lady Grizel Boyle and the Hon. Mrs D'Arcy Hart."

Posh young women stepped out of the pages of Debretts to model clothes for the catalogues.

"Weather permitting, Lady Donatia intends wearing her gown at Ascot." Society came no higher.

"Lady Plummer bought some gay silk parasols and Princess Ottobons chose a black scarf."

The celebrated flyer, Amy Johnson, was a guest at one show.

Jack Buchanan, the debonair film star, bought a dressing gown at another.

The Daily Mail nominated the Claridges' Sale 'The event of the season' as over 2,500 people turned up.

In all this 'hobnobbing', as she called it, Mrs Carter had an invaluable ally in Captain Lionel Scott, Painted Fabrics financial chief. He knew the right people – and if he did not know them he knew how to get to know them.

"It was what one did during the summer season in those days: Ascot, Henley, Wimbledon and Painted Fabrics sales"

Annie Bindon Carter never lost sight of her credo of 'work not charity' and the moral imperative for Painted Fabrics to be a proper business.

In this respect Mrs. Carter was supported by the most respected authorities in the field.

As Ruskin suggested at the time:

"All works of taste must bear a price in proportion to the risk, expense, skill and time attending their invention and manufacture.

These things called are, when justly estimated, the cheapest and the dearest attended with much less profit to the artist than those which everyone calls cheap.

Beautiful forms and compositions are not made by chance, nor can they in any material be made at small expense.

Competitions for cheapness and not for excellence of workmanship are the most frequent and certain causes of the rapid decay and entire destruction of Arts and Manufactures. "

Sold on quality

Brochures and sales descriptions enticed and intrigued potential buyers with vivid and detailed descriptions of design subjects and stories, fabrics and materials used and product ranges, including:-

'Coarse linen wall hanging backed in blue cotton; stencilled and painted; depicts Queen Elizabeth I and the words 'Saint Elizabeth, Princess Elizabeth'

'Green silk tablecloth, stencil printed; border edged with images of grapes, flowers and apples and centre panel depicts maypole, galleon and Elizabethan dance pageant.'

'Satin church cloth with calico hem at top added for display pole to be inserted, stencilled and painted, depicts angels and cross with grapes order.'

'Two satin curtains/hanging panels with stencilled borders edged with flowers; shields and check depicting George and the Dragon.'

'Silk and satin alter cloth edged with padded piping, lined with green satin and silk tassels in the top left hand corner; stencilled, printed and painted, depicting angels and the words 'Mercy and Truth are met together, Righteousness and Peace have kissed each other.'

'Coarse linen wall hanging stencilled and painted; depicting King Henry VIII, Wife and Cardinal Wolsey and the words 'Who hath my heart truly be sure and ever shall.'

'Decorated curtains and banners, featuring 'Indian' designs and English pottery designs – work completed in Wharncliffe Hospital during the first World War.'

'Theatrical hangings, theatre stage sets, Anthony and Cleopatra, Merchant of Venice.'

'Tapestry at St. Anne's Church, Sheffield.'

'Curtains and lunette at the studio of Ethel M. Eadon [Photographer].'

'Curtains in the Long Gallery at Wentworth Castle.'

'Hangings supplied to a London house.'

'Curtains designed and dyed for St. Martin's Church, Windermere.'

'Mural for Maud, Countess Fitzwilliam, Wentworth Castle.'

'Wooden Church altar made out of derelict aeroplanes used in the War and constructed by the men stationed at the Norton Aerodrome, pictured at Southwell Minster, Nottinghamshire.'

'Coarse linen wall hanging, green silk tablecloth, satin church cloth with calico hem [display pole], satin curtains/hanging panel, silk and satin altar cloth.'

Much more than 'ladies in stencilled dresses' on offer!

Some efforts were made at more conventional advertising appropriate to the times and the target audiences, particularly through the medium of the 'Sasmarian', including:-

"A very natural impression exists that only painted, printed or patterned silks can be obtained from us. We certainly specialise in the decoration of material, but as we manipulate these silks ourselves from the raw state, we have always in stock a big selection of dyed and finished undecorated silks, and we are only too pleased to supply plain undecorated silks in an attractive colour range to our customers, if desired. Please write for a colour chart and a sample of material."

"We find the modern spirit in Sasmarian merchandise showing artistic vision and imagination at its best coupled with sound craftsmanship. Our materials are the best obtainable; each finished article is an individual work of art. They cannot therefore be 'cheap' in the price sense of the word, but they are certainly cheap in the sense of value for money." Nothing like blowing your own trumpet!

"We have showrooms in Marcol House, 293 Regent Street, London W1, and no-one will assume that you wish to make a purchase unless you suggest it yourself. We are only too pleased to send a selection of things on approval at any time to any of our old customers or to any of our new customers on receipt of the usual references."

"We have our own dressmaking service and we are pleased to make up any of our materials on order at prices much lower than the average, owing to the fact that we run this department without profit, using it simply as a means of selling more material as people will often not buy at all if they cannot have it made up." This approach to business might be called 'diversification' by an organisation in a 'differentiated' phase of organisation development in modern business school jargon, but it does show how sophisticated the business approach of this remarkable organisation and its management had become after so little time and experience."

And on price...

Painted Fabrics sold its goods in an open market where its special circumstances counted for nothing. Its prices had to be competitive.

PRICE LISTS in the 1930s included a wide range of items:

• Cushion covers [25inches square], £1–9s–6d,
• Chair backs [pair], £1–5s–6d,
• Bedspread [3yards by 2 yards], £6–6s–0d,
• Curtains [pair 3.5 yards x 50 inches], £11–11s–0d,
• Satin and Moire Taffeta Bedspreads, £6–16s–6d,
• Rest Gowns, £7–17s–6d,
• Night Dresses, £3–3s–0d,
• Pyjamas, £3–18s–6d,
• Mappie Coats [Kimonos], £5–5s–0,
• Shawls [painted], £6–6s,
• Shawls [printed], £3–13s–6 d.

The show must go on

Jennifer Murray was the great niece of Annie Bindon Carter and she offered her services at exhibitions and sales.

'There was a big sale at the Cutlers Hall in Sheffield. The British actor Jack Buchanan came to open the sale. He looked around and decided to buy a Painted Fabrics dressing gown for his wife, but he wanted to see what it looked like on, so I had the honour of wearing it – then he bought it'.

The illustrated brochure and price list for 1930 included an overview of the company; a detailed price list of furnishings; novelties and dress goods; photographs of products; terms of business; and photographs of men employed.

These Sales and Fairs were important events in the Painted Fabrics calendar, but involved an enormous amount of work for a relatively un-sophisticated organisation compared to the well-known fashion houses of the Metropolis and Regional centres. Venues had to be booked, sponsors arranged, invitations sent out, and publicity arranged:-

"Sale of work at the Cutlers' Hall, Sheffield, Christmas Fair 5th to 13th December 1933 – thanks to the Master and Mistress Cutler for opening the fair."

There were also special fabric sales and fêtes.

The Star Wednesday 9th November 1949 announced:-

"Royalty to Open Yule Fair"
"The Princess Royal will make the first sale and the Lord Mayor, Alderman Mrs. Grace Tebbutt will make the first purchase at the Christmas Fair of Painted Fabrics in the Cutler's Hall, Sheffield on Friday, November 25th.
The event is being organised jointly by the Painted Fabrics Soldiers and Sailors Mutual Aid Association and the Council of Social Service for their respective funds.
Two thousand invitations have been sent out for the first opening ceremony to be performed by the Princess who is patron of the Painted Fabrics Association.
The fabrics have been painted and processed by ex-servicemen of two World Wars."

The below from the Sheffield Star in 1939 was in fact not the last sale but rather the latest in a long line.

"LAST SALE"

"Princess Royal acted as stallholder at the last sale of fabrics painted by Sheffield disabled ex-servicemen in 1939 when she was assisted by Lady Fitzwilliam.

The Lord Mayor, who will be acting as chairman at the opening, will be accompanied by the Lady Mayoress, Mrs. Olive Barton.

The Mistress Cutler, Mrs. W.R.S. Stephenson, will be hostess and the Master Cutler, Mr Stephenson, will also be present.

The opener of a second ceremony, to which the public will be invited, will be announced later. Amongst the disabled who will sell the Painted Fabrics goods, painted at the Meadowhead work rooms, will be the youngest recruit of the Sheffield Association, 23 year old Cyril Owen, who lost both legs when a German tank ran over him during the crossing of the Rhine."

"Fabrics for sale on the Princess's stall will include a dressing gown in white slipper satin, stencilled with roses, a dressing gown in black chiffon velvet, similarly stencilled, and a large variety of cotton handkerchiefs."

Covering the country

Exhibitions and sales were not only Painted Fabrics' main selling outlet, they were extensively used to promote the ethos and moral purpose of the whole exercise and involve the local communities in the far-flung places where events were held, right up to the end.

The Bolton Exhibition of 1951 began by using our old friend William Wallwork – "a local Bolton man" – and the local newspaper to drum up interest.

As reported in the Bolton Evening News 6th April 1951:-

"Painted Fabrics was formed during the 1914-18 war as a result of a meeting between Mrs Carter and a Bolton man who had both hands amputated.

The only means of selling articles made at the centre is by holding exhibitions and sales up and down the country.

It is proposed to have an exhibition and sale in Bolton in June and many of the townswomen's organisations have promised to take charge of a stall.

Those who attended a meeting on Tuesday last were shown some of the attractive fabrics and articles which have been painted at the centre.

Bolton women will be responsible for paying the wages of several ex-servicemen for a few weeks after June 1st, representatives of most of the town's women's organisations were told that they had this responsibility at a meeting convened by Bolton W.V.S in the town hall. Speaker at the meeting was Mrs G.C. Carter M.B.E, founder of Painted Fabrics, a national organisation which provides employment and homes for disabled ex-servicemen at the centre in Sheffield."

After the event it was reported that:-

Bolton Evening News 1st June 1951

"An Exhibition which set Bolton housewives flocking to the Town Hall today was that by disabled ex-servicemen of Painted Fabrics. The name is quoted purposely because that is the name of the War Charities' Organisation in Sheffield where disabled war veterans apply their skill to the colourful, exacting work of making curtains, dressing gowns, scarves and other manufactured goods into something more than the standard article obtainable in the local department store. Mr W.A Grierson, who opened the exhibition, said that this was a splendid example of the way in which local organisations got together to remedy matters neglected by the state. The Government had failed to provide sufficient means for the welfare of ex-servicemen, but here in Bolton women were doing their best to remedy that by organising this exhibition of work by the Sheffield centre.

Throughout the day the exhibition continued to welcome intending buyers, and women stall-workers combined the duties of mannequin and saleswomen as they displayed beautifully painted dressing gowns, scarves and other apparel. From the beginning it was evident that this Exhibition was a deserved success."

Painted Fabrics on parade

Exhibitions were announced splendidly as:-

"Exhibitions and sale of exquisite Fabrics and other merchandise by war disabled craftsmen working under the direction of skilled fashion artists and designers."

Guests were also promised 'Mannequins will parade at 3.00 and 4.00pm'

At the Greenacres Showroom (Johannesburg, South Africa), Sir Frank Benson's South Africa Exhibition was held.

Exhibitions in London included:-

Tuesday November 27th 1951 as reported in the Sheffield Telegraph with the headline:- *"DISABLED SOLVING PRESENT PROBLEMS"*

"When the Queen visited a recent exhibition in London of work done by disabled ex-servicemen, one of the purchases she made was a bedspread in thick material with a satiny finish and a delightful floral pattern. The bedspread was just one of the lovely things made at the Painted Fabrics factory, Meadowhead, Sheffield, by the totally disabled ex-servicemen who live and work there. Christmas is the busiest time for these workers. The pretty things they have been making for Christmas have to be finished off and packed up for various exhibitions of work." Mrs G.C. Carter, the founder of Painted Fabric,s told the Sheffield Telegraph yesterday that they were hoping to sell £2,000 worth of goods before the end of December."*

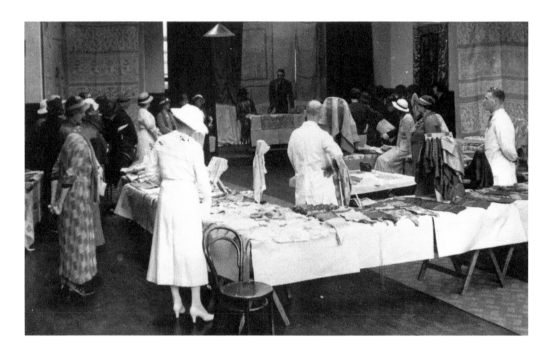

Poodle Design

She also reported, "Crêpe handkerchiefs were one of the more successful lines which the factory is turning out this year.

 A novel design is a border of little black poodles on a white or pink background, or if you prefer, a giraffe printed in delicate colours.

One well-loved design which the factory is using again this year is the square headscarf with a deep scalloped edge which makes it less bulky to tie around the head or throat.

The men have not been forgotten, and presents for husband or sweetheart would be a silk scarf or handkerchief.
Other lines in which the factory specialises includes shopping bags, dressing gowns and gaily-patterned aprons."

Shopping, shopping, shopping

Printed Fabrics gift shop on the corner of Fargate and Leopold Street, Sheffield (open for one month).

6

Here for Life

– In Good Company

Painted Fabrics became a centre for refuge and treatment, a well-run business, an internationally-known fashion house – and a thriving community.

All the communities were where Painted Fabrics established itself after the first efforts to help had been started in the Wharncliffe War Hospital were successful to a degree, but Painted Fabrics final home at Meadowhead is where everything came together. New premises had been established at Shalesmoor in the centre of town, then on the southern outskirts at Coal A, but ever ambitious, they did not provide the opportunity to bring everything and everyone together that Mrs Carter was looking for.

Finally Little Norton Lane, Meadowhead, became the place where Painted Fabrics finally settled and began to fulfil its potential as a fully-integrated working and living community. Annie Bindon Carter's dream which she had had from the humble beginnings at Wharncliffe War Hospital began to come true.

The men we take we regard as being here for life

The Little Norton Lane, Meadowhead, site lay at the top of one of Sheffield's many hills on the edge of the South West suburbs, with Graves Park at the back and overlooking the Sheaf Valley below. The main road to Dronfield and Chesterfield passed by and Meadowhead tram terminus marked the end of the long climb up the hill from Heeley Bottom.

Painted Fabrics is still remembered to this day with a sheltered housing scheme occupying the original Little Norton Lane site and with a permanent exhibition in the local Weston Park Museum.

At its peak Painted Fabrics provided facilities for over 60 families.

It soon became well known locally as the place where:-

"They all sang old Army songs as they worked and called the place 'Eden.'"

Long after the First World War was over, disabled soldiers continued to be referred to Painted Fabrics as its reputation grew, not as an art house but as a place where help could be provided for ex-servicemen with severe injuries of a quality and kind which could not be obtained anywhere else. Not all were from Sheffield but they quickly became part of the community.

The residents of Painted Fabrics

Arthur Fisher's story

When he was discharged from hospital, Arthur and his fiancé Annie (nee Bell) were married at Walkley Parish Church in 1919. Hadfields had offered Arthur a post for life, however he went to work at Painted Fabrics.

After they were married the wedding car pulled in at the bottom of the old drive and they walked up it with everyone clapping.

Arthur and Annie lived at No 3 Painted Fabrics and their daughter Nancy was born there in 1923.

Nancy Fisher married Herbert Blackburn in 1944. Herbert was in the RAF. They later had a daughter Christine.

William Wallwork's tale

Phyllis Lawton uses the story of William Wallwork as a proud example of the way that lives were transformed at Painted Fabrics and how this process of transformation continued over an extended period of time – "for life", in fact, all facets of personal, work, family and community life included. The story of Pte. Wallwork she tells so movingly exemplifies the completeness of the Painted Fabrics story.

"When Painted Fabrics became a peacetime industry, Wallwork was one of the first to work for them, but his father was in a quite good position and bought him a poultry farm, so he went back to his home town – Bolton, I think.

When the Duchess of York visited I was puzzled about something familiar about a man in ordinary clothes [Painted Fabrics always wear white coats]. He was rather like Wallwork, but surely this smartly-dressed, well set up man, looking very fit and alert, couldn't be. He looked confident, sure of himself and happy. I was incredulous, amazed – then I saw him take a handkerchief from his pocket with his teeth and I knew. I hastily pushed my way through the quickly gathering crowd and went up to him, and he didn't remember me until I mentioned a certain cushion cover, a little mauve stencil on crash which I had assisted him with so long ago. He looked remarkably fit and I was delighted to see him again. I saw him later in Annie Carter's car with his wife. They were her guests for the day."

Building a community

During the first years that Painted Fabrics started, men were recruited from all over the country:

M. Ashworth from Derby,
F. Scott from West Yorkshire,
J. Street from Hampshire,
A. Ellis from Suffolk,
H. Gregory from Middlesex,
T. W. Williams from Wales,
G. Ramsey from Worcester,
A. Richards from Scotland,
J. Bull from Manchester.

They all quickly became proud citizens of Painted Fabrics.

Family life was very important to Painted Fabrics, as Arthur (Fisher) became bedridden in the last years of his life and Nancy would often be seen pushing him in his wheelchair to Graves Park to play bowls.

The British Limbless Ex-Servicemen's Association (B.L.E.S.M.A) granted Arthur a specially adapted Morris Minor car a few years before he died, but as he was not well enough to drive it for long a nephew would drive him out in it. Some of his favourite places to visit were Blackpool and Boston in Lincolnshire, where he used to enjoy sitting by the river.

Arthur Fisher died on the 29th November 1957 aged 73 and Annie died in April 1985 aged 91. Both are buried in Abbey Lane Cemetery.

Arthur was still living at Painted Fabrics when he died with Annie staying there until the mid-1960s when she was rehoused in a council flat. Her final years were spent in an old people's home.

Mrs Carter regularly told her audiences with great pride:-

"Beside the men who work there are those now too old to work, widows, wives, children and a few married children of older workers."

Community spirit

"There was a terrific sense of community, with local entertainers, actors and singers being brought in for Christmas parties and the like."

During one visit Mrs Carter told her guests:-

"Every encouragement and assistance is given to the young people who are growing up.
- One boy is apprenticed to a dentist.
- Two boys who are 14 only are sitting for their matriculation.
- One girl is an elementary school teacher.
- One girl is a typist.
- One girl is a domestic servant.
Some other girls who are old enough are working in the making up department at Painted Fabrics itself."

Regular events were held in the community with the wives and children of Painted

Fabrics employees involved at weddings, children playing in the gardens and the houses on the estate and children modelling Painted Fabrics clothing. Everyday village life carried on.

The men showed their ability to work together as a team and show capacity for physical efforts seemingly far beyond their capabilities. When a temporary hut was accidently set on fire, in a few moments the amateur fire fighters were on the spot with hose and appliances. The difficulties presented by their maimed limbs were deftly ignored and this experience clearly showed how the men had been trained to be ready in case of danger during their time at the front, but this skill was now being applied in a very different way in their new community setting.

Painted Fabrics in the community

Distinguished people from the wider Sheffield community were represented at Painted Fabrics and were regular visitors. For example, Betty Owen, organiser of the Sheffield Municipal Progressive Party, organised sales for Painted Fabrics, and Dr Rothenstein, Director of Sheffield Art Galleries and later the Tate Galleries in London, was on the advisory committee of Painted Fabrics.

Being part of the wider Sheffield community was an advantage when it came to fundraising with outside bodies. When the Douglas Haig Memorial Homes application was made in 1928, it was noted:-

"The fact that you are in the vicinity of a large town and are definitely giving employment to the men, who would live in the cottages proposed, weighs very much with the trustees. I may also note that in order to make our money go as far as possible we are desirous of helping communities on the pound-for-pound basis – that is to say, if Sheffield locally would raise half the money required, we would find the other half."

As a result the new Haig homes were built.

Part of the scenery

There were soon requests for help received from the immediate local Sheffield community as word 'got round' of what Painted Fabrics were 'up to'. Local people looked to Painted Fabrics as a source of possible help for their own from one of their own.

Heeley Vicarage,   *July 14th 1929*

My dear Mrs Carter,
I am writing to you on behalf of a disabled ex-serviceman who I understand has applied repeatedly for the last 15 months to Painted Fabrics for employment and residence. One leg is amputated and the other leg is badly affected by osteomyalitis. His name is Mr E. Parkin, 55 Heeley Green, Heeley. I would be grateful if you could do something for him or give me some message of encouragement to him.

The Painted Fabrics site was an open house with anyone and everyone welcome to visit and see what was going on, right from the start. You never could tell, after all they might become a supporter, a volunteer or a sponsor. At any rate they would spread the word locally and perhaps further afield about what a wonderful job they were doing.

All were welcome, from workmen working at the site on the new developments, to tradespeople and suppliers, volunteers and staff, council officials and people on company official business. Visitors came often for fêtes, galas, visiting days and special ceremonies; weddings, birthdays, christenings and anniversaries; Christmas and New Year celebrations, Bonfire night and when United won the cup (not often!). Every kind of dignitary and class of hoi polloi from royalty downwards visited – and quite a few nosy parkers too no doubt. All succeeded in putting Painted Fabrics firmly on the map.

The Painted Fabrics community had been described, rather disparagingly, by some cynical hack as consisting of "Allotments, Brownie Packs and vegetable shows."

At other times local newspapers were quick to point out a more pleasing and attractive, aspect of life at Painted Fabrics, reporting how important visits were organised and daily life on the site was represented.

"Painted Fabrics is a familiar institution to the people of Sheffield, but its cause is not widely known as it should be. It was started in Sheffield in a humble way shortly before the end of the War with the objective of providing work for severely disabled men who could otherwise follow no occupation, and their goods of high-quality designs and colour schemes have already made their reputation."

In 1952 the News Chronicle reported:-

"Now Painted Fabrics is a community of 48 families living in its own houses around workshops, where beautiful hand-dyed and hand-patterned textiles are made by happy men with a purpose in life."

A special occasion

Painted Fabrics always tried to make the most of the special events and occasions which came its way to project its purpose and image – and its need for support.

On 26th July 1926, the Morning Telegraph reported:-
"The men here do their own gardening, including digging. Some kneel – one man uses a specially constructed spade, with a special loop fitted to the top of the foot of the spade and a strap attached to the handles. The damaged hand guides the spade, the foot pushes it into the ground, then the action of the foot and the strap around the neck withdraws the spade and turns same over.

Along the corridor, past the houses where mothers, babies and young children were assembled at the bottom of the drive and to inspect the proposed site for the Earl Haig Memorial Homes."

In 1952 The News Chronicle reported:-
"Now Painted Fabrics is a community of 48 families living in its own houses around workshops, where beautiful hand-dyed and hand-patterned textiles are made by happy men with a purpose in life."

Long after Painted Fabrics had closed, a former editor of the Star recalls receiving regular correspondence on a variety of topics and subjects from a gentleman whose address was Painted Fabrics, Little Norton Lane, the former site of Painted Fabrics, showing that right up to the present day Painted Fabrics remains an integral part of the wider community of Sheffield.

7

Learning and Legacy

Back to the future

In some ways Painted Fabrics was an enigma, a paradox, a curiosity and an anachronism – but it worked.

Most of the soldiers for whom it was set up came from the working class. The Privates were largely from the poverty-stricken, desolate industrialised East End, the N.C.Os from business, officialdom and trade occupying the in-between areas before the leafy suburbs and 'posh' areas of the South West. Sheffield Painted Fabrics was located on the edge of the more affluent, middle- and upper-class suburbs of the West Side of the city which eventually reached out to the stately homes and old money of the Peak District and Derbyshire. In this part of the world geography delineated class quite clearly and precisely, but Painted Fabrics always seemed to be difficult to define and pin down, representing everybody yet nobody in particular.

To add to this conundrum of contrasts, the support and sponsorship upon which Painted Fabrics so clearly relied came predominantly from further out still: from the gentry, nobility and eventually the royalty of the nation, involving the places they lived and the way in which they lived. Yet Painted Fabrics' main supporter, there right from the beginning, Maud Fitz, had her stately home in the middle of a South Yorkshire coalfield!

Painted Fabrics perhaps shows us that it might just be possible to transcend the usual barriers and limits of social status, money and wealth, power and position for a just cause rooted firmly in the soil of a common humanity.

The sad, tragic truth is that we did not learn much from the horrors of the Great War, and seemingly our most recent conflicts. Hence the continuing need for organisations such as Help for Heroes as governments throughout the world periodically go through the sickening ritual of wringing their hands in remorse and regret (but never admitting any blame) for the events and consequences of war, before embarking seemingly blindly into the next gut-wrenching adventure.

A place of work

'Work not Charity' was Painted Fabrics' slogan, an ambition carried on by organisations such as Remploy to the present day. What was different about Painted Fabrics was its insistence on becoming a local, legitimate, limited company, dedicated to employing one specific set of men and fitting in to its own defined business, economic and social background.

To go from the destruction and abdication of WWI to the creativity and dedication of Painted Fabrics involved a transformation based on re-establishing what was good and overcoming the negative effects and consequences of the conflict.

Maintaining the comradeship of the war in peacetime and demonstrating that people could work together towards a common purpose and a positive outcome involving subtle co-ordination of the combined efforts and purposes of artists and engineers, designers and craftsmen, sales and production, finance and gardening, building towards a creative, durable and sustainable end.

COMMON CAUSE and COMMON PURPOSE,
LIONS SERVED BY DONKEYS,
WOMEN BY MEN,
MEN LED BY WOMEN.
ALL LED BY ANNIE BINDON CARTER

The Croft, Malton, North Yorkshire
15th February 1957

My very dear friend, dearest Binnie,

"Bless you and thank you for your lovely letter, all most interesting and I loved hearing about Painted Fabrics. It is sad it has come to an end — but what a truly wonderful work you have completed, and so many lives you have made happy, and who, without you would have been so sad and no interest left, with nothing to do and nothing to look forward to accomplishing and producing something worthwhile. The curtains [made at Painted Fabrics] still hang at Wentworth Castle and here the bedspread to match, which all came from the shop at Chesterfield Street. What happy days were the exhibitions at Wentworth and No 4 Grosvenor Square and then at Claridges to which the Princess Royal drew the King's attention.
I do congratulate you from the depths of my heart. Bless you and much love."
Maud Fitz, Countess Fitzwilliam

The final act - winding up the business

Painted Fabrics finally closed its doors after 40 odd years in 1959.
One of the final matters of business which had to be attended in many ways sums up the main focus and purpose of this remarkable initiative and the people who guided and cajoled it to success and achievement — the welfare and well-being of the men they had accepted a duty of care towards — within the context of a thoroughly responsible approach to business matters, of course.

"At a meeting held on Wednesday 20th August 1959 the following resolutions were accepted:-

1. It was agreed to accept Mr Wolf's proposed value of stock and pay purchase tax on this valuation which would most likely be assessed at approximately 50 per cent under possible selling price.

2. It was agreed that Mr Landon should write to Brookes and Bownes and inform them that the committee had agreed to pay each one a pension of 4 pounds per week until they reach the age of 65 or previous death providing the finances of the Company are available."

Annie Bindon Carter was still at the helm when the business closed. At the end severely disabled servicemen were still employed making a range of goods from as it had done since she and her small group of art students, started their work to help soldiers returning from the First World War battlefields in France and Belgium decades earlier.

After the Second World War there were similar cases of disablement to deal with but by that time the authorities were much better-placed to provide appropriate care and rehabilitation, and medical science and equipment design had advanced rapidly.

The Star and Garter Home, Richmond, Surrey
10th February 1942

Dear Mrs Carter

I have been in rather a doubt about writing to you, but when my wife told me you had been there on Xmas morning it rather took the doubt away and you know how I want to keep PAINTED FABRICS still very much in my thoughts. Because I shall never forget what a real good pal everyone was to me, especially at the end of my working days, when everyone was so very kind. So you understand what a soft corner Painted Fabrics holds in my heart.
Well, Mrs Carter, how are you these days? I do hope that you are still keeping that cheery smile on, because it used to be something to see in the middle of work, a dear, pleasant face.
I am pleased to say I am keeping very good health myself at present but I've had a rotten three months.
Oh, Mrs Carter, there is some new I'd almost forgotten to tell you, we have a new commandant now, our old one has been stricken with the same complaint as us, so he has to spend the rest of his time in a wheelchair.
Remember me to all at Painted Fabrics.
J. Llewellyn [Taffy] DCM

The last Sheffield lad to fall at the Somme

My Pal Denver Smith and I both sing Baritone in the Bolsterstone Male Voice Choir. He is very much a Sheffield lad from Hillsborough way, himself severely disabled by polio from infancy. In early 2014 along with countless others he and I made a trip to Northern France and Belgium to mark the 100 years since the start of the Great War.

We travelled together, latter-day Sheffield Pals, on a long-delayed trip to the battlefields of Flanders, especially to visit the tiny village of Serre, in the Somme, where the Sheffield Pals Regiment had been slaughtered in 1915. As we made our way to the graveyard and memorial the skies darkened and the heavens wept.

In order to reach the memorial and graveyard we had to negotiate a tricky descent of some 200 yards, on a muddy track across the grassy fields. We should not have set off, but we had come a long way and we knew what we had to do. No sooner had we attempted to make a move across the soaking wet grass than his walking stick slipped and down he went. I lifted him up and took him back to the car. With few words said, he then took out the small wooden cross complete with poppy he had been given, gave it to me and I walked gingerly down the now muddy track to the cemetery and placed it carefully on the grave of a 'fallen' soldier of the Sheffield Pals. On it was inscribed "From one Sheffield lad to another."

His mission had been to place the cross on a grave, and he had carried it all the way from Sheffield, and he was not going to fail now.

Later I pointed out to him that the 2014 Tour de France route would be passing through the Somme battlefields on the 100 year memorial of the start of the 1914–18 War.

"I know," the modern day Sheffield Pal said,

"Remember I was the last Sheffield lad to fall at the Somme!"